Elite • 239

Armies of the Iran–Iraq War 1980–88

CHRIS McNAB

ILLUSTRATED BY STEPHEN WALSH

Series editors Martin Windrow & Nick Reynolds

OSPREY PUBLISHING
Bloomsbury Publishing Plc
Kemp House, Chawley Park, Cumnor Hill, Oxford OX2 9PH, UK
29 Earlsfort Terrace, Dublin 2, Ireland
1385 Broadway, 5th Floor, New York, NY 10018, USA
E-mail: info@ospreypublishing.com
www.ospreypublishing.com

OSPREY is a trademark of Osprey Publishing Ltd

First published in Great Britain in 2022

A catalogue record for this book is available from the British Library.

ISBN: PB 9781472845573; eBook 9781472845580;
ePDF 9781472845559; XML 9781472845566

22 23 24 25 26   10 9 8 7 6 5 4 3 2 1

Map by Alan Gilliland
Index by Rob Munro
Typeset by PDQ Digital Media Solutions, Bungay, UK
Printed and bound in India by Replika Press Private Ltd.

Osprey Publishing supports the Woodland Trust, the UK's leading
woodland conservation charity.

To find out more about our authors and books visit
www.ospreypublishing.com. Here you will find extracts, author
interviews, details of forthcoming events and the option to sign up for our
newsletter.

Acknowledgements

We would like to thank Eric H. Larson, one of the editors of camopedia.org
(a website dedicated to the categorization and history of camouflage
patterns, a valuable and unusually comprehensive resource for anyone
researching the subject); his expertise, reassuring in its breadth and freely
given, was an important contribution to the accuracy of this book's
artwork. In terms of source material, special acknowledgement goes to E.R.
Hooten, Tom Cooper and Farzin Nadimi for their four-volume work *The
Iran–Iraq War*, which constitutes one of the most detailed technical and
tactical studies of this conflict.

FRONT COVER, ABOVE: Iranian Revolutionary Guards rejoice atop their
BMP-1 infantry fighting vehicle, following their victory over Iraqi troops on
24 January 1987 on Bovarian Island, located near the port of Basra, Iraq,
during the *Kerbala 5* offensive. Items of civilian clothing are worn alongside
military dress. (ERIC FEFERBERG/AFP via Getty Images)
FRONT COVER, BELOW: Iraqi soldiers engage in a firefight with Iranian
troops along the Iran–Iraq border in July 1984. The Iraqis are wearing
standard khaki combat dress with M80 helmets and a variety of local and
foreign-made load-bearing equipment. (Jacques Pavlovsky/Sygma via
Getty Images)
TITLE-PAGE PHOTOGRAPH: Iranian Basij personnel of all ages, wearing
bandannas reading 'Karbala Pilgrims', assemble in the Azadi Stadium in
Tehran on 7 February 1986, before departing for the front. One of the
Iranian slogans during the eight-year war was 'We will be in Karbala'. This
Iraqi city, some 100km south-west of Baghdad, is a holy city for Shi'ite
Muslims. (Kaveh Kazemi/Getty Images)

Artist's note

Readers may care to note that the original paintings from which the colour
plates in this book were prepared are available for private sale. All
reproduction copyright whatsoever is retained by the publishers. All
enquiries should be addressed to:

info@stephenwalsh.co.uk

The publishers regret that they can enter into no correspondence upon
this matter.

CONTENTS

INTRODUCTION   4

IRAN–IRAQ WAR CHRONOLOGY   6

THE IRANIAN ARMY   8
Structure and organization ▪ Recruitment and training ▪ Front-line service

THE PASDARAN   16
Structure and organization ▪ Recruitment and training ▪ Front-line service

THE BASIJ   22
Structure and organization ▪ Recruitment and training ▪ Front-line service

IRAN'S OTHER PARAMILITARY FORCES   28

IRANIAN WEAPONRY AND EQUIPMENT   29

THE IRAQI ARMY   34
Structure and organization ▪ Recruitment and training ▪ Front-line service

THE IRAQI REPUBLICAN GUARD   44
Structure and organization ▪ Recruitment and training ▪ Front-line service

IRAQI PARAMILITARY FORCES   53
The Iraqi Border Guard ▪ The Popular Army ▪ National Defence Battalions

IRAQI WEAPONS AND EQUIPMENT   57

CONCLUSION   60

FURTHER READING   62

INDEX   64

ARMIES OF THE IRAN–IRAQ WAR 1980–88

INTRODUCTION

Somewhat overshadowed by the 1967 Six-Day War, the 1973 Yom Kippur War, the ending of the Vietnam War in 1975 and Operation *Desert Storm* in 1991 – not to mention the concurrent Soviet war in Afghanistan (1979–89) – the Iran–Iraq War (1980–88) has been rather marginalized in modern military history. On every level, however, this is intellectually unwarranted, for it was arguably the largest and longest purely conventional war since 1945. Indeed, some authorities plausibly contend that it was the last conventional war, in the sense of one fought and decided via the head-on clash of mass infantry and armoured formations. Fought over a grinding eight years, it inflicted anywhere between 1 million and 2 million casualties, including possibly 500,000 dead soldiers. It also generated 2.5 million refugees and reshaped the balance of power in the Middle East. Few other conflicts in the post-1945 era rival the Iran–Iraq War for its prolonged human and social impact.

The triggers for this seismic conflict were predictably complex: a mixture of long-standing territorial and border disputes between Iraq and neighbouring Iran, accentuated by deep ethnic and religious tensions and galvanized by the characters of the two countries' leaders, Iraq's Saddam Hussein and Iran's Ayatollah Ruhollah al-Musavi al-Khomeini (known to the West as the Ayatollah Khomeini). The key elements that fuelled the outbreak of hostilities included Iraq's ambition to take control of the oil-rich province of Khuzestan, located on the Iranian side of Iraq's south-eastern border, plus its equal desire to control both banks of the Shatt al-Arab (River of the Arabs) that separated the two countries, and which provided Iraq with its principal access point to the Persian Gulf. Iraq also felt threatened by pre-revolutionary Iran's huge military and economic expansion, made all the more tangible by Iranian encouragement of Kurdish separatist revolts in Iraq in 1974–75. Thus Saddam spotted opportunity in the disruptions and military weakening in Iran caused by the Islamic Revolution of 1979, and in September 1980 he ordered his forces to invade Khuzestan province, with the aim of capturing the important Iranian city of Khorramshahr. Saddam was not interested in a war of conquest – rather he stopped his forces a short distance inside Iran and hoped to achieve his goals politically. Iran went on the counter-offensive, pushing the Iraqis back across the border and continuing the war into Iraq itself.

So began eight years of bloodshed. Much of it was a dreadful and static border conflict, punctuated by periodic offensives involving human-wave

assaults and pounding artillery exchanges. Both sides launched air and missile attacks on opposing industrial facilities and rival-flagged oil tankers, and Iraq even resorted to the open use of chemical and biological warfare. For much of the conflict, Iran appeared to hold the advantage, even capturing Iraq's vital al-Faw Peninsula in February 1986; but while Iraq garnered the international support of the West, the Arab world *and* the Soviet Union, Iran became a virtual pariah state, its armed forces steadily withering through underinvestment and casualties. In 1988, Iraq returned to the offensive, retaking the al-Faw Peninsula in April and re-entering Iranian territory in mid-July. This led to Iran accepting UN Resolution 598 on 17 July 1988 (Iraq followed suit the next day), bringing about a ceasefire which came into effect on 8 August, and subsequent peace talks resulted in the conflict finally ending on 20 August.

In this book, we focus not on the history of the conflict, but the land armies that shouldered the brunt of the fighting and the losses. Studying these armies also aids our understanding of why the Iran–Iraq War was both so long and so costly. The armies of Iran and Iraq had their growth and development shaped by many influences – external powers, revolutions, internal strife, international wars, Cold War ideology, religion, ethnicity and economics – but an overarching consideration is that both armies had a deeply *political* relationship to their supreme leaders and the ruling parties. Both Saddam Hussein and the Ayatollah Khomeini, despite being worlds apart in ideology, shared a rather binary attitude to national military forces, viewing them as means of keeping and projecting power while at the same time being suspicious of future rebellion emerging from their ranks. This is one reason why both Iran and Iraq created alternative land forces to the regular army, as loyal counterweights.

ABOVE LEFT
7 February 1986: a member of Iran's Basij paramilitary organization attends a rally in the Azadi (Freedom) Stadium in Tehran before his departure for the front. (Kaveh Kazemi/Getty Images)

ABOVE RIGHT
Iraqi troops smile for the camera, 1 May 1988. Here we see the basic khaki combat dress of the Iraqi soldier, with a fly-fronted shirt with two breast pockets (concealed buttons) and trousers with large thigh pockets. (Thomas Hartwell/ The LIFE Images Collection via Getty Images/Getty Images)

IRAN–IRAQ WAR CHRONOLOGY

1980
23 Sep	Iraqi forces invade Iran, beginning the Iran–Iraq War
22–24 Oct	Iraqi forces besiege Abadan and capture Khorramshahr

1981
5–11 Jan	Iranian counter-offensive around Susangerd fails
27–29 Sep	Operation *Thamin al-Aimma*: Iran breaks siege of Abadan
29 Nov–7 Dec	Operation *Jerusalem Way*: Iran captures Bostan

1982
22–30 Mar	Operation *Undeniable Victory*: Iranian offensive pushes Iraqi forces back in Dezful–Shush area
24 Apr–25 May	Operation *Jerusalem*: Iran occupies most of Khuzestan province and liberates Khorramshahr
13 Jul–2 Aug	Operation *Ramadan*: five failed Iranian offensives to capture Basra
1–10 Oct	Operation *Muharram*: four Iranian offensives in Amara area, for small gains

1983
6–16 Feb	Operation *Before Dawn*: failed Iranian offensive in the southern sector in the Musian area
10–17 Apr	Operation *Dawn*: failed Iranian offensive near Amara
22–30 Jul	Operation *Dawn 2*: Iranian offensive in Kurdistan advances 14.5km inside Iraq
30 Jul–9 Aug	Operation *Dawn 3*: failed Iranian offensive in the region of Mehran
20 Oct–21 Nov	Operation *Dawn 4*: Iranian offensive in the northern sector penetrates a few kilometres into Iraq

1984
7–22 Feb	First 'war of the cities'
15–24 Feb	Operations *Dawn 5* and *Dawn 6*: massive Iranian offensive along a 240km front between Mehran and Bostan
24 Feb–19 Mar	Operation *Khaibar*: Iranian offensive towards Basra; failed, but captured Majnoon Island
18–25 Oct	Operation *Dawn 7*: limited Iranian offensive on the central front

1985
28 Jan–early Feb	Failed Iraqi offensive on the central front around Mehran
11–23 Mar	Operation *Badr*: failed Iranian offensive towards Basra
22 Mar–8 Apr	Second 'war of the cities'
Jul	Iranian operations in Kurdistan

1986
6–10 Jan	Iraqi attack on Majnoon Island
9–25 Feb	Operation *Dawn 8*: Iranian offensive on southern front; al-Faw Peninsula captured
14 Feb–3 Mar	Operation *Dawn 3*: indecisive Iranian offensive in Kurdistan
30 Jun–9 Jul	Operation *Karbala 1*: Iran recaptures Mehran

31 Aug	Operation *Karbala 2*: Iranian offensive in Kurdistan
1–23 Sep	Operation *Karbala 3*: Iranian offensive around al-Faw Peninsula and Majnoon Island
24–26 Dec	Operation *Karbala 4*: Iranian offensive towards Basra

1987
9 Jan–25 Feb	Operation *Karbala 5*: failed major Iranian offensive towards Basra
14–18 Jan	Operation *Karbala 6*: Iranian offensive in the Sumar area
17–25 Jan	Third 'war of the cities'
Feb–Apr	Fourth 'war of the cities'
12 Feb	Operation *Fatah 4*: Iranian operation in Kurdistan
7 Mar	Operation *Karbala 7*: Iranian offensive, Haji Omran area, Kurdistan
6–9 Apr	Operation *Karbala 8*: Iranian offensive towards Basra
9 Apr	Operation *Karbala 9*: Iranian offensive in the Qasr-e Shirin area
8–22 Oct	Increasing clashes between Iran and United States in the Persian Gulf

1988
29 Feb–30 Apr	Fifth 'war of the cities'
15–16 Mar	Iraqi forces kill thousands of Kurdish civilians with chemical weapons in the town of Halabja
19 Mar	Iranian forces attack Bubiyan Island
18 Apr	Iraqi forces recapture al-Faw Peninsula
25 Apr	Iraqi forces recapture territory around Shalamcheh
25 Jun	Iraqi forces recapture Majnoon Island
13–17 Jul	Iraqi forces enter Iranian territory, before withdrawing and making a peace offer
20 Aug	Ceasefire and subsequent peace talks bring Iran–Iraq War to an end

A painfully young Iranian soldier of the Basij, wearing a bandanna and a helmet cover with Koranic verses emblazed upon them. Imbued with revolutionary fervour and confidence in a paradisiacal afterlife, the Basij incorporated soldiers below the age of 18 in its ranks, although they contributed little other than being targets for Iraqi guns and mines. (Mohammad Hossein Heydari/GFDL/Creative Commons)

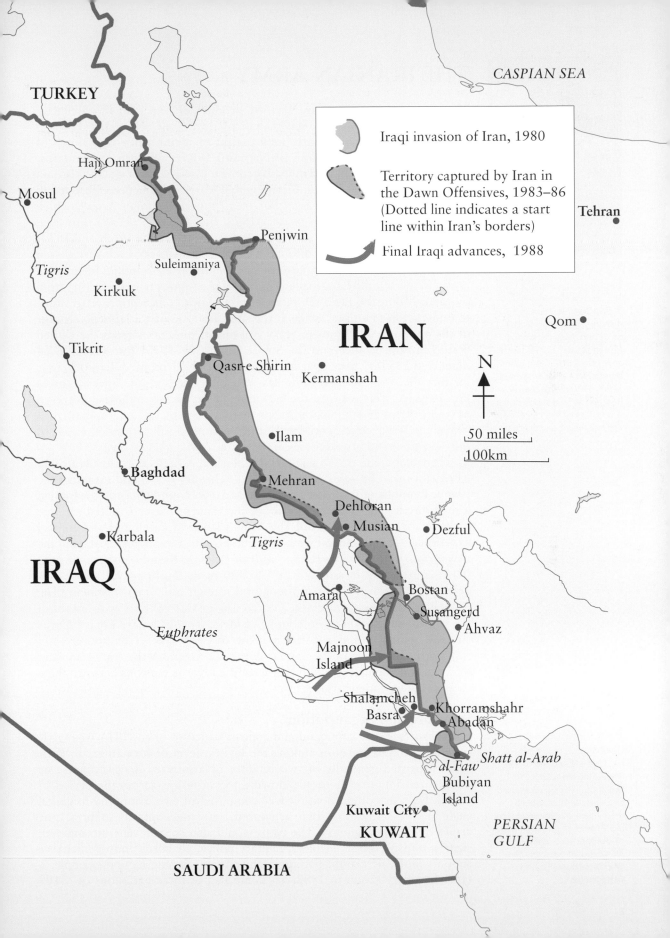

CASPIAN SEA

TURKEY

Mosul

Haji Omran

Tigris

Kirkuk

Tikrit

Penjwin

Suleimaniya

IRAN

Tehran

Qom

Qasr-e Shirin

Kermanshah

Ilam

Baghdad

Mehran

Dehloran

Musian

Dezful

IRAQ

Karbala

Tigris

Amara

Bostan

Susangerd

Ahvaz

Euphrates

Majnoon
Island

Shalamcheh

Basra

Khorramshahr

Abadan

Shatt al-Arab

al-Faw

Bubiyan
Island

Kuwait City

KUWAIT

*PERSIAN
GULF*

SAUDI ARABIA

N

50 miles
100km

Iraqi invasion of Iran, 1980

Territory captured by Iran in
the Dawn Offensives, 1983–86
(Dotted line indicates a start
line within Iran's borders)

Final Iraqi advances, 1988

THE IRANIAN ARMY

Southwestern Iran, April 1964: an Iranian soldier moves up during Exercise *Delawar*, a joint military exercise conducted by US and Iranian personnel. He appears to be armed with an M1 Garand rifle and wears the standard khaki field dress, with a US M43-type blouse and trousers bloused into the boots. (Francis Miller/The LIFE Picture Collection via Getty Images)

The pre-1979 Iranian Army was the product of one man in particular, Mohammad Reza Shah Pahlavi, Shah of Iran from September 1941 to February 1979, a particularly long period of incumbency. For much of the 20th century, oil-rich Iran (Persia until 1935) had been manipulated, coerced and frequently controlled by foreign powers, most notably Britain and Russia/the Soviet Union. Britain would leave its influence embedded in the *Qushun-i Muttahid al-Shikl dar Iran* (Imperial Iranian Army), which was formally established in January 1922. In the post-1945 era, however, foreign authority over Iranian affairs weakened, and in the 1960s and 1970s the Shah was able to force through a comprehensive set of reforms, driven heavily by his desire to make Iran the dominant economic and military power in the Middle East, made possible by prodigious riches resulting from oil sales. Militarily, the Shah introduced a major conscription programme to boost soldier numbers while at the same time sinking a large percentage of the nations's GDP into military equipment purchases from the United States, Britain, France and the Soviet Union. By 1979, Iran's land army numbered 285,000 men, distributed between three armoured divisions, four infantry divisions, and two infantry, one airborne and one Special Forces (SF) brigades. This was just the beginning of the Shah's ambition, however, as within Iran's 39 million population there were potentially 5.1 million men who could be called to arms. For a time, the Iranian military stood as one of the most powerful armed forces in the whole of the Middle East.

Then came the 1979 Islamic Revolution, which saw the Ayatollah Khomeini take the reins of power on 1 February 1979 and establish the Islamic Republic of Iran. The revolution had a profound effect on the Iranian armed forces. The officer class above the rank of major suffered a purge of its senior strata, weakening the Army's stock of command-and-control experience. Compounded by extensive desertions, the purges resulted in the new *Artesh-e Jimhuri-ye Eslami-ye Iran* (Islamic Republic of Iran Army; IRIA) contracting in strength to 100,000 men; the upheaval also had a deleterious effect on skills, training and foreign military investment. The Ayatollah Khomeini's attempted corrective to this effect was to establish his faithful revolutionary militia, the Islamic Revolutionary Guard Corps (IRGC), which would eventually grow to even greater manpower and superior influence than the regular Army. Throughout the Iran–Iraq War, the Iranian campaign would be compromised by the tensions between these two near-independent armies.

Structure and organization

On the surface, the command-and-control structure of the IRIA was fairly traditional in composition. Taking the highest level of formation, an IRIA corps consisted generally of two infantry or armoured divisions and one mechanized infantry division (allowing for variation across the period of study). Each armoured division was composed of two armoured brigades, each of five battalions: two armoured, one mechanized infantry, one artillery and one engineers. The corps would also contain separate engineer, signals, transportation, artillery, military police, air corps and maintenance support units, at group, battalion or company strength. For example, a typical artillery group in 1982 was composed of three battalions of M109

self-propelled (SP) howitzers, one battery of M107 SP howitzers, four battalions of towed artillery and one Multiple Launch Rocket System (MLRS) battalion.

By the midpoint of the war, the total strength of the IRIA was 45 brigades, of which 16 were armoured/mechanized formations, 24 infantry, and five SF or airborne. The major constituents were: the 16th, 81st, 88th and 92nd Armoured divisions; the 21st, 28th, 30th, 58th, 64th, 77th and 84th Mechanized Infantry/Infantry divisions; the 23rd Special Forces Division; the 37th Armoured Brigade; the 40th Infantry Brigade; and the 45th Special Forces Brigade (Hooten et al. 2017: 31–33).

A further significant element of the Iranian ground forces was the Islamic Republic of Iran Army Aviation (IRIAA). At its peak strength this consisted of 1,000 helicopters, divided into three cavalry divisions and five air groups. This branch of service provided the IRIA with some degree of airmobility and rotary-winged aerial artillery, although tactical misuse and underuse meant that this asset was frequently squandered.

Although the IRIA retained its traditional combat structure on the surface, in terms of command and control much had changed since the Islamic Revolution. Now the IRIA was under the closest political and ideological scrutiny, emanating from the Ayatollah Khomeini himself, who occupied the peak of the hierarchy as the military commander-in-chief. Directly below him was the Supreme Defence Council (SDC), which included the Iranian Prime Minister, the Minister of Defence, the Chief of the Joint Staff, the IRGC commander-in-chief, and two representatives appointed specifically by the Ayaltollah Khomeini himself. The SDC both oversaw and worked with the armed forces Joint Staff who distributed commands to regional operations HQs, which from there went down to task force HQs.

The efforts of the SDC meant that every stratum of Iranian military society was under the repressive and close scrutiny of the theocratic regime. As part of the SDC, the SDC Secretariat – a large body of staff manned by politically reliable senior clerics – posted individuals to every major command organization to oversee the political reliability of command staff and to ensure that every major decision was aligned with regime policy and the Ayatollah Khomeini's will. There were, however, further levels of micromanagement.

IRIA commanders were kept under watch by the Political–Ideological Directorate (PID). Like the SDC, the PID was staffed principally by clerics, and it was responsible for implementing policies relating to political propaganda and indoctrination. The scrutiny provided by the PID's sub-organizations extended its control down to the lowest levels of the IRIA. The PID Secretariat kept watch over the Joint Staff and corps and regional operations HQs. The Political Ideological Branches (PIBs) had authority within divisional, brigade and battalion commands, while personnel from the 'Strike Groups' were distributed right down to platoon level, ensuring that political control extended from the very top to the very bottom of the IRIA.

Recruitment and training

In the aftermath of the 1979 Islamic Revolution, the IRIA was immediately subjected to a purge by the new regime, one that removed those military personnel who were perceived as not aligned with the new theocratic vision or who appeared too connected with the values and politics of the former Imperial Iranian Army. The officer class bore the brunt of the purge: 77 high-ranking IRIA officers were executed, including 26 generals, and up to 23,000 more personal were removed by 1986, about 12,000 in the first year of the revolution. Revolutionary transformation encouraged thousands more skilled military personnel to leave the ranks; the IRIA dropped to a manpower strength of just 100,000 by mid-1980, a huge haemorrhage of personnel. The rise of the Pasdaran, which drained willing recruits away from the regular Army, also contributed to the depletion of the IRIA.

The result was a severe skills shortage within the IRIA, particularly in relation to operating advanced machinery and weaponry, plus the associated

The single yellow chevron on this Iranian soldier's sleeve indicates that he is a 3rd sergeant. There are four sergeant ranks in the Iranian military, beginning with sergeant (which is preceded by private, private 2nd class and private 1st class) then going through 3rd, 2nd and 1st sergeant; the next most senior enlisted ranks are warrant officer II and warrant officer I. The motif on the helmet is the national emblem of the Islamic Republic of Iran, adopted in July 1980 and consisting of four crescents (a stylized representation of the word 'Allah'), in overall shape similar to that of a lotus flower and also a tulip (a symbol of martyrdom) with a central sword surmounted by a *shaddah* diacritical symbol. (Laurent MAOUS/Gamma-Rapho via Getty Images)

problems of over-promotion of junior officers, who were also given responsibilities far beyond their experience and pay grade. The problems were compounded by the loss of staff at officer training colleges, and also by the fact that many of the specialist foreign advisors and equipment specialists left the country after the Islamic Revolution.

Officer recruits under the new regime were preferably of more fundamentalist Shia religious backgrounds, especially those with strong connections to reliable clergy. (Both Iran and Iraq are majority Shia, but in Iraq the country's ruling class were Sunni, who constituted about 30 per cent of the population.) There was also a new leaning towards recruiting officers from the lower and middle classes, as opposed to the upper-class bias of the imperial army. The lower ranks of the IRIA were fleshed out via the 18-month conscription of 18–45 year olds, instituted by the Ayatollah Khomeini, plus the use of festival-like 'Armed Forces Days' to encourage military volunteerism. To accelerate and encourage recruiting, the conscription period was later reduced to 12 months and a concession was made by which conscripts were permitted to serve within their home provinces. A significant problem with the high volumes of new recruits was that of illiteracy, which ran at a rate of about 60 per cent in the wider country. To make the conscripts functional, therefore, the IRIA had to train many of its recruits to read and write, an effort that led to a 10 per cent improvement in the national literacy rate by 1986. For the IRIA, however, the Pasdaran's increasingly voracious claims on Iraq's manpower meant it frequently fell short of its recruitment quotas. The majority of the men who joined the IRIA only received training in light-infantry roles, with extremely little in combined-arms manoeuvres. Most men of the IRIA therefore entered battle severely undertrained; training regimes frequently focused more on installing unthinking discipline rather than front-line initiative.

Front-line service

The experience of the IRIA front-line soldier during the Iran–Iraq War was characterized by austerity interspersed with relatively frequent exposure to bursts of violent combat. Front-line nutrition, for example, was basic and often unpredictable, mostly consisting of simple soups, stews, cheese, flat breads (baked in mobile field bakeries), some fruit and, rarely and deliciously, some meat. Equipment was similarly unimaginative. The infantry largely fought the war with small arms and light support weapons such as machine guns and mortars, occasionally and generally imperfectly coordinating their efforts with armour and artillery (see below).

One of the biggest problems for both sides during the war was the endless struggle against environmental conditions, particularly heat, dust and rare torrential rains, the latter turning dusty plains into viscous muddy landscapes. The heat and the dust in particular caused problems in maintaining weaponry and sensitive equipment such as radios. Even tank gun barrels would warp in the midday heat, while the temperatures inside armoured fighting vehicles (many of which had been designed with Soviet and northern European winters in mind) could rocket to 54°C, quickly inducing heatstroke and dehydration among those inside.

Apart from the environmental concerns, the troops of the IRIA also paid the price of underinvestment and tactical mismanagement. Like many Arab armies during this period, the IRIA was highly centralized in its tactical thinking, discouraging the low-level tactical initiative that was by this time

Oshnavieh, Iran, 1 January 1986: accompanied by his aides, an IRIA officer briefs the media on the activities of Iranian forces fighting in northern Iraq. The three stars on his shoulder straps indicate that he is a *sarhang* (colonel), with the crossed rifles on his collar denoting infantry. (Photo by Kaveh Kazemi/Getty Images)

commonplace in Western armies. This frequently, although not always, made the IRIA tactically leaden, and prone to unimaginative human-wave frontal attacks (see the section on the Pasdaran below) that produced grotesque levels of casualties. During Operation *Karbala 4* in December 1986, for example, some 200,000 Iranian troops, 40 per cent of whom were IRIA personnel, attacked along the Shatt al-Arab towards Basra in a fruitless 39-hour drive that gained no territory but cost up to 12,000 Iranian dead and wounded, compared to 3,000 Iraqi casualties.

Iran's tactical problems were compounded by frequently poor coordination between infantry, armour, artillery and air power, particularly in offensive operations that required efforts to be synchronized across time and space simultaneously. Combined-arms operations need intensive investment in training, united command and control, and an excellent communications infrastructure to implement effectively, and all too often the IRIA and other elements of the ground forces had none of these convincingly in place. In many ways, however, the Khomeini regime's enthusiasm for martial spirit and theological enthusiasm over considered tactics reduced the level of the problem in their thinking, at least in the first half of the war

There were many other problems besides for the IRIA. It lacked mobility for offensive operations, and its logistics train was generally inadequate; several major offensives burned out partly because logistics could not extend themselves over a long penetration. There were also command clashes between the IRGC and IRIA, leading to a dissipation of effort and the IRIA being tactically sidelined by the more dominant Pasdaran. Finally, the Iranians generally had poor operational security. By the time they launched Operation *Karbala 4*, for example, both the Iraqi Army and the Iraqi Air Force were totally cognizant of the fact that the attack was on its way, and were on full alert, with hundreds of artillery guns positioned and ready to meet the Iranian attack. Of course, over such a long war there were many localized cases of Iranian forces showing initiative and cooperation in combined-arms operations, but they were not common enough to stops hundreds of thousands of lives being squandered in the dust and sand.

A IRANIAN ARMY INFANTRY

(1) Sergeant, Khorramshahr, September 1980

The *Gruhban Sevom* (sergeant, 2nd class) wears the standard M62 helmet; Iran purchased many thousands of the M62 during the 1970s from the West German Bundeswehr, although in Iranian use there was some adaptation, particularly in colouration (many Iranian helmets were painted in a sand colour) and through the use of locally made chinstraps, liners and mesh nets. He also wears a domestically produced version of the US OG-107 utility uniform – all three patterns of the OG-107 shirt and trousers can be found in the Iranian forces or the period, and though some might have been acquired through deals for surplus stock or as third-party commissions, it is likely that the vast majority of such uniforms were produced within Iran by a number of different manufacturers working to varying standards and requirements. Such a system made for a variety of different styles within the broad arc of the three main OG-107 patterns, with differences in the cut, pockets, buttons, shoulder straps all being common. His boots are an Iranian version of the US M67 and his belt is a copy of the US M56, but his webbing and ammunition pouches are of Israeli manufacture, a large amount of such materiel (including weapons) having been imported prior to the fall of the Shah. He carries the standard weapon of the Iranian infantry throughout the war, the 7.62×51mm G3A6 battle rifle.

(2) Machine-gunner, 21st Infantry Division, 1982

The soldier is moving with his MGA3 machine gun, a heavy weapon at 10.5kg, not counting the reams of ammunition that it could tear through so rapidly. He wears the M62 helmet with a camouflage uniform in one of the numerous French vertical 'lizard'-pattern variations that had been issued to some units in the pre-revolutionary army. Such designs may have come directly from France, but it is more likely that the influence originated with Israel, where notable users of the 'lizard' pattern included paratroopers and other elite units throughout the 1950s–70s. Across all the different branches of the Iranian armed services, a particularly wide and at times extremely colourful range of camouflage styles could be seen: 'brushstroke' patterns dating from the imperial period; British Disruptive Pattern Material (DPM); and US M1942 spot-pattern camouflage, known as 'Panther' camouflage, this pattern and the 'brushstroke' patterns often being seen with wide colour variations. This particular uniform is in the style of OG-107 shirt and trousers, but with a different base material, and like the olive-green version it is domestically produced. The MGA3 (the Rheinmetall designation given to the licensed and Iranian-produced version of its MG1A3) is a post-war evolution of the infamous MG 42 general-purpose machine gun that was redesigned to chamber 7.62×51mm NATO ammunition in the late 1950s–early 1960s. The MGA3 uses a short-recoil system, fires from an open bolt, is air cooled and belt fed, and has a rate of fire of up to 1,200rd/min. It has an integral bipod for its role as a light support weapon, but can also be mounted on a tripod for use as a heavy machine gun. The quick-change barrel, one of the weapon's original design features, allowed an expert crew to swap in a new barrel in six seconds, but it was unlikely that most of the Iranian MGA3 crews had sufficient experience or training to achieve such feats.

(3) Soldier, 28th Infantry Division, Operation *Dawn 4*, 1983

This infantryman wears an M17 protective mask. As the war progressed, Iraq would use more sophisticated nerve agents in its chemical attacks, but in the earlier years mustard gas was the most likely chemical weapon that would be deployed against Iranian positions. The soldier, like many of his compatriots, lacks full protective gear such as the US-produced Mission Oriented Protective Posture (MOPP) suits, instead relying on his protective mask alone; the M17 was a robust and effective American design that was the standard-issue protective mask for US forces from the 1960s until the 1990s. The mask found widespread use within the IRIA, though due to the suspension of military trade between the US and Iran in the wake of the Islamic Revolution, its numbers had to be supplemented by a variety of other models sourced from several third parties. The soldier wears a standard utility shirt, but with trousers in a green variant of 'Panther' camouflage, the Iranian term for the style derived from the old American M1942 spot-pattern camouflage, popular in one form or another since the 1970s. He carries an Iranian-made M1 Garand bayonet as a fighting knife, and a battered G3A6 battle rifle as his main weapon.

THE PASDARAN

On 5 May 1979, the Ayatollah Khomeini formally established the *Sepah-e Pasdaran-e Enghelab-e Eslami* (Islamic Army of the Guardians of the Islamic Revolution), or simply *Pasdaran*. This force was intended as an ideologically reliable counterweight to the pre-revolutionary forces that still formed the core of the Iranian military, and an army unto itself that was religiously motivated, loyal to the Ayatollah Khomeini in person, and under tighter clerical control. In January 1981, the Pasdaran took the official title Islamic Revolutionary Guard Corps (IRGC), part of a continual phase of growth in manpower that transformed the Pasdaran into *the* most powerful element of the Iranian ground army. As its ranks grew, so did the IRGC's centrality in the front-line war.

It is worth remembering that the Pasdaran was not the Ayatollah Khomeini's invention. *Pasdar* (Guards) paramilitary units came into existence early in the Islamic Revolution, in the form of extremist Islamist groups centred around influential local warlords and leaders. Indeed, in many ways the Ayatollah Khomeini's creation of the IRGC was his attempt to control the decentralized and factional nature of the *Pasdar*, a situation that was actually never fully resolved throughout the conflict. Local IRGC units might have as much loyalty, and in some cases arguably more, to the proximate cleric or commander than to the Ayatollah Khomeini, who sat distant in Tehran.

The role and evolution of the Pasdaran has been plausibly likened to that of the Waffen-SS in Hitler's Germany during the 1930s and 1940s (Schahgaldian 1987: 73). Like the Waffen-SS, the IRGC grew from a significant but still relatively minor bodyguard organization to a land army of hundreds of thousands of men. Its purpose, according to the Islamic Revolution's new constitution, was to guard the Revolution and its achievements both ideologically and militarily through a a fusion of military force and internal policing, all conducted through pure theocratic vision. Aside from the IRGC's military role, the organization also conducted a wide range of supplementary national duties, including: enforcing Islamic laws and rules; combating counter-revolutionary factions; conducting intelligence (i.e.

Iranian Revolutionary Guards, armed with G3A6 battle rifles, are pictured near Qasr-e Shirin, Iran, very close to the border with Iraq, in October 1980. The soldier at centre wears Israeli-made khaki load-carrying equipment, and has an IRGC chest patch on his left tunic pocket. (Kaveh Kazemi/ Getty Images)

Iranian Revolutionary Guards, clearly defined by their red bandannas, gather in Imam Hossein Square in Tehran on 16 May 1985. The actions of the Pasdaran on the front line were often highly dramatized and glorified in the Iranian press, to encourage further volunteerism. (Kaveh Kazemi/ Getty Images)

spying) operations among the population; propagating authorized religious and political doctrines; and recruiting people for military or civic service. The sheer logic and demands of war between 1980 and 1988, however, compelled the IRGC to frame itself more exclusively as an army.

Structure and organization

As with the IRIA, the Ayatollah Khomeini had ultimate authority over the Pasdaran, via the SDC. Looking at the IRGC structure in 1985, the main command body was the IRGC Central Command, run by the IRGC commander-in-chief, who was appointed (or dismissed) directly by the Ayatollah Khomeini. The next step down in the chain of command was the regional commands, of which there were 15 by 1987, corresponding to provincial remits. The regional commands were subdivided into district commands, then base commands, then barrack commands (Schahgaldian 1987: 78). At its administrative and political levels, the IRGC also had 15 sections each with a specific area of interest. These were: Personnel and Administration; Planning and Supervision; Operations and Training; Intelligence and Research; Tribunal Section; Security Unit; Reconstruction Unit; Special Operations; Cultural Activities; Women's Affairs; Public Affairs; Religious Training; Logistics and Support; Procurements; and Disaster Unit. Although headquartered in Tehran, these organizations were still relevant to the wider IRGC, as they had representatives placed within regional and district offices.

The bulk of the front-line IRGC was made up of 26 infantry divisions, each consisting of about 6,500 men, plus 43 independent brigades of about 1,400 men each. Each infantry division consisted of 12 infantry battalions, one artillery battalion, one heavy support battalion, a reconnaissance battalion and a company-sized engineer battalion (Hooten 2017: 32). Other major combat units deployed to the front included two armoured/ mechanized divisions, one armoured and two mechanized brigades and six engineer divisions, plus multiple artillery, anti-armour, air defence, engineer and (later) chemical decontamination brigades. The Pasdaran also had naval infantry units, which eventually totalled five brigades of Marines and SEAL-type operatives, plus coastal-defence artillery (Hooten et al. 2018: 32).

Recruitment and training

The IRGC's growth in manpower speaks volumes about its role in the Iranian armed forces in general. In May 1979, the Pasdaran had just 4,000 members in its ranks, but by the end of the year that figure had more than doubled to 10,000. By June 1981 it had reached 25,000, but with the official establishment of the IRGC the subsequent growth was exponential. By 1983 it had 150,000 men, 250,000 by 1985, 350,000 by 1986 and 500,000 at its peak in 1987–88.

This epic expansion was fuelled both by an intensive recruitment drive and enthusiastic queues of volunteers. We should not only ascribe religious ardour to the growth trajectory, however. During the 1980s Iran was gripped by severe unemployment (2–3 million people did not have work), and the Pasdaran offered both a stable income (its pay rates were better than those of the IRIA) and social status for many disenfranchised young men. Indeed, as the war progressed, such practical motivations would often be the primary reason for enlisting; US intelligence analysis from the 1980s noted that by 1986 the horrors of war had diluted ideology as a primary cause of military service, as evidenced by the increasingly strict monitoring of spirituality in the ranks by government-appointed clerics.

The focus of recruitment to the IRGC had fairly tight channels. The ideal recruit was 18–26 years old, unmarried, poor and urban (i.e. young men with little to lose). This demographic brought with it problems for an army that was gradually trying to professionalize itself, hence later in the war the IRGC made more of an effort to recruit college graduates and professionals, who were capable of taking on more specialist roles. The ranks of the IRGC had strong leanings towards Shia Persians; Sunni Muslims and non-Muslims had a low representation, although they were not entirely absent.

Recruitment and command in the IRGC often centred around the local efforts of influential clerics and leaders. One effect of this was not only to form local power bases within the IRGC, but also to shape the flow of recruitment, as a RAND Corporation analysis authored by Nikola

Soldiers of the Pasdaran prepare to go into action in 1982. Part of the IRGC logo (a stylized arm gripping a weapon, the weapon itself being out of view here) can be seen on the helmet of the soldier to the left. Koranic verses painted onto helmets, webbing straps and firearm slings were common. The uniform camouflage – black, green and red 'island' patterns set on a tan background – tended to be worn by the IRGC and the Basij on the south-western front. (Laurent MAOUS/Gamma-Rapho via Getty Images)

Schahgaldian and published in 1987 reported. The analysis posited that the fragmented, factional nature of the IRGC spurred rival power bases to boost their own standing by recruiting as many members as possible, a process accelerated by the drive to mobilize the population in support of the war effort. Moreover, entire family groups or clans would be enlisted at the behest of their leaders, and then serve together (Schahgaldian 1987: 71). The regional and tribal factors influencing IRGC recruitment produced something of a suicidal competition, with local IRGC leaders proudly proclaiming their victory in volumes of martyrs produced. This disdainful view of casualties distorted Iranian tactics for at least the first half of the war. Yet as Schahgaldian points out, the factionalism within the IRGC was ultimately not destructive to the overall organization, which developed its own umbrella sense of identity, particularly in relation to the other Iranian arms of service.

Because of its ideology-first persuasion, however, IRGC training was largely inadequate. During the initial years of the war, a Pasdaran warrior might receive just two weeks of basic infantry training before being transferred to the front line. The overwhelming focus of training was on infantry assaults with basic weapons, accompanied by intensive classroom programmes of theological indoctrination; but over time, as tactics improved somewhat, the training improved in quality and scope. At first, the Palestine Liberation Organization (PLO) helped established training programmes in major urban areas such as Tehran, Ahvaz and Qom, but by the mid-1980s the IRGC had more professional training centres dotted around the country, including some run jointly with the IRIA, IRIAF and the Islamic Republic of Iran Navy (IRIN), which in turn led to efforts to conduct joint military exercises. Up to the very end of the war, however, technical expertise among the IRGC's ranks remained scarce, exacerbated by the fact that many technical manuals were in English and that there was a serious shortage of qualified instructors.

ABOVE LEFT
15 February 1986: members of the Iranian Revolutionary Guard operating in the al-Faw Peninsula use a backpack radio set. Note the gas mask carried at the ready. In anticipation of chemical raids by Iraqi aircraft, Iranian military personnel were equipped with gas masks and NBC gear after the Iranians launched a surprise attack against the Iraqi troops defending al-Faw. (Kaveh Kazemi/Getty Images)

ABOVE RIGHT
15 February 1986: a fatigued-looking member of the Iranian Revolutionary Guard is depicted with smoke rising behind him over the Iraqi oil installations in the Al-Faw Peninsula. He is wearing a Chinese-type chest rig to carry his battle-order ammunition and equipment. (Kaveh Kazemi/Getty Images)

Front-line service

While the general conditions of service for the IRGC were little different from those of the IRIA, tactically there were some significant differences. Units of the IRGC and the Basij (see below) became famed for their use of frontal human-wave assaults, throwing their bodies openly onto the barrels of Iraqi defensive firepower in a simple effort to overwhelm by mass. In the first half of the war, this tactic was apparently pursued with some enthusiasm – IRIA soldiers remember witnessing IRGC warriors stepping up for the assault, smiling and joking and with a relaxed demeanour. Although the IRGC employed crude tactics, the high levels of motivation among its personnel, their willingness to close and fight, was deeply threatening to both Iraqi infantry and armour, and the aggression of the Pasdaran was key to many of Iran's major victories during the war.

The human-wave approach was, predictably, enormously wasteful of life, not helped by poor coordination with IRIA armour and artillery. As the war progressed, therefore, changes were implemented. From *c*.1984 there was a conscious effort to reduce the reliance on human-wave tactics. In training and doctrine the IRGC therefore began to focus more upon infiltration, patrolling and reconnaissance, as well as the core practices of fire and manoeuvre. The IRGC also took advantage of low-light and night-time conditions to make attacks, and they started to integrate more with neighbouring IRIA units, thus improving combined-arms capabilities. Yet these improvements were not enough to prevent Iraqi firepower eliminating a sizeable proportion of the IRGC's manpower.

B

PASDARAN AND BASIJ FORCES
(1) Missile operator, 5th *Nasr* Division, 1987

The *Sarbaz Adih* (private) wears an M62 helmet displaying the rank marking of a private soldier in the Pasdaran, simple running shoes and an Iranian-produced uniform based on the style of the US OG-107 shirt and trousers (1st pattern), but in the domestic camouflage design known as 'Panther', originally derived from the US M1942 spot pattern. He carries a 7.62×39mm AK-63D assault rifle, a Hungarian copy of the Soviet AKMS, but his main weapon is the M47 Dragon ATGM slung across his back, its sight carried in an M67 shoulder bag. The M47 entered US service in 1975, with a certain number purchased by Iran prior to the Islamic Revolution; the system was made up of two parts – a disposable launching tube and a detachable sighting system. The Dragon had a minimum firing distance of 75m and a maximum range of 1,500m, though in reality 1,000m was the limit of its effective reach when engaging stationary targets, with a range of 100m for enemy vehicles that were on the move. This relatively short range was considered a serious drawback by the US Army, but for the Iranians the M47 proved to be effective and it was widely used, especially in the earlier years of the war. The M47 was a man-portable, shoulder-fired wire-guided weapon that used a SACLOS (semi-automatic command to line of sight) targeting system – the SU-36/P Daysight and AN/TAS-5 Nightsight for day and night operation respectively – that required the operator to maintain his view of the target until the missile hit home. The weapon had a notable report when fired, as well as a back-blast area of 50m, making the location of the operator an open secret. The main projectile was the M222 HEAT round that was capable of penetrating 2.4m of packed earth, 1.2m of reinforced concrete and 330mm of steel

plate (the most modern iteration of the T-62 main battle tank's turret frontal armour was 242mm thick).

(2) Basij volunteer, 1981

The zealous young Basiji wears an M62 helmet with a martyrdom band affixed, and a 'brushstroke'-pattern camouflage uniform that was associated with Basij volunteers and other IRGC units; it came in several variations and was informally known as *Atishi* (fire) or *Shahid Hemmati* (Martyr Hemmat, after a commander who had died in the war) pattern. Two significant distinguishing features of the Pasdaran were the wearing of a red or green bandanna, inscribed with verses from the Koran. (Sometimes the bandannas might be visually represented by painted stripes on the helmet.) They would also wear a wooden or plastic key on a cord around their necks, symbolizing the keys to heaven itself. In the early years of the war, many IRGC soldiers were seen going into action without wearing their helmets, such was their belief in the liberty of God to decide what to do with their lives. Later in the war, however, helmet-wearing seems to have become a more common practice. His equipment is simple, consisting of little more than a domestically produced three-cell chest rig and his weapon, a 7.62×39mm Zastava M70B1 assault rifle, a Yugoslavian copy of the Soviet AKM, captured from Iraqi forces in an earlier battle.

(3) Major, 33rd *Al-Mahdi* Division, 1984

The *Sargord* (major) wears a simple dark-olive field cap, such headgear being common in a number of designs made from both plain and camouflage material, and a rare 'puzzle spot'-pattern camouflage uniform, only worn by members of IRGC and Basij units. He also wears a British Pattern 58 belt and holster for his US 9×19mm Browning Hi-Power pistol, a trophy taken from a captured Iraqi officer.

THE BASIJ

While the IRGC garnered a reputation for fanatical self-sacrifice, even this was somewhat overshadowed by another organization within its remit, the *Sazeman-e Basij-e Melli* (National Mobilization Organization), usually referred to by its *Basij* shorthand. Actually, the full name of the Basij had been through a colourful evolution, as in September 1980 it became the *Sazeman-e Basij-e Mostazafin* (The Organization for the Mobilization of the Deprived), which turn later became the *Vahed-e Basij-e Mostazafin-e Sepah-e Pasdaran-e Enghelab-e Eslami* (The Mobilization Unit of the Deprived of the Islamic Revolution Guards Corps), when it was placed under the command authority of the IRGC at the end of 1980.

During the Iran–Iraq War, the Basij, which at times included children barely into their teens, became renowned for its personnel's unnerving willingness to advance openly and with no tactical finesse across minefields and into Iraqi defensive firepower, consequently suffering enormous and often preventable casualties. Like the Pasdaran, the Basij was the expression of the Khomeini regime's attempt to create forces that were identifiably and ideologically loyal to the regime. It was formed in November 1979, as part of the Ayatollah Khomeini's vision for a 'people's army of 20 million' to be raised to defend the new Islamic Republic of Iran against internal enemies. The original Basij was loosely conceived, however, and subject to competing perceptions about its role, which ranged from the establishment of a major new internal security force to an army committed to the struggle against US imperialism. Initially it didn't even have its own dedicated budget. Then came war in late 1980, and it was clear that the Basij would have a role to play, hence it was eventually brought inside the IRGC structure.

A young member of the Basij proudly stands with his AKM-type assault rifle. He wears a collection of uniform items, all of which appear too big for him, including an M56-style belt, a US-type water-bottle and cover (of 1940s and 1950s design) and some improvised webbing. (Mohamad ESLAMI RAD/Gamma-Rapho via Getty Images)

Tehran, 7 February 1986. Basij personnel chant anti-US slogans while holding AK-47 assault rifles aloft, during an assembly in the Azadi Stadium in Tehran before departing for the front line with Iraq. The uniforms are a mix of whatever surplus items were available, including a military parka-style coat (far left), a chemical-warfare jacket (second left) and combat shirt (third left). Many men of the IRIA and even of the Pasdaran were less than impressed by the Basiji, viewing them as amateurs making pointless sacrifices, although other soldiers appreciated the way they drew the heat of Iraqi fire away from others. (Kaveh Kazemi/Getty Images)

Structure and organization

Within the IRGC, the Basij was controlled by the Central Basij Council (CBC) in Tehran, headed by the Basij commander, who was appointed by the IRGC commander-in-chief and monitored by a 'supervisor' appointed by the Ayatollah Khomeini. The IRGC Central Staff would also take control of major operational matters. Lower down, the Basij was divided into operational areas led by regional field commanders, with the force separated into divisions, resistance bases, resistance districts and resistance groups. There were also various administrative HQs in Iran.

A sub-organization within the Basij was the *Basij-e Ashayer* (Tribal Mobilization), formed in September 1980. This organization operated in Iran's tribal regions, where it was tasked with diverse duties such as recruiting and training tribal people for military service, collecting supplies for front-line troops, conducting operations against anti-regime factions and warlords, and coordinating indoctrination programmes.

This extraordinary photograph shows the profound age contrasts within the ranks of the Basij. These particular members are participating in an exercise in Robat Karim outside Tehran in 1988. Their uniforms are a hybrid of civilian clothing and whatever pieces of military uniform they could acquire. (Kaveh Kazemi/ Getty Images)

Recruitment and training

Like the Pasdaran, the Basij went through a rapid expansion in its numbers. By the end of 1982 it consisted of about 400,000 volunteers, serving through some 9,000 active cells, which in turn were anchored to more than 6,000 'resistance bases' connected with local mosques. By 1985, the number of resistance bases had grown to 10,000 and the claimed number of trained Basiji to 3 million, although 'only' about 600,000 served in actual front-line roles (Schahgaldian 1987: 94).

The individual Basiji were mainly volunteers, albeit ones motivated and recruited from within mosques and revolutionary organizations. The ideal profile of a Basij warrior was a poor, uneducated, but ideologically motivated young man of between 18 and 30 years of age, although far younger members – down to and below the age of 14 – were also accepted into the ranks. Unlike the Pasdaran, many members of the Basij were from the rural rather than urban poor, and many of them were illiterate. Those who could read and write hoped to enter the Basij's administrative organs, and a steady and respectable middle-income job. Significantly the Basij also recruited women, despite the Islamic regime's views on women's place in society, using them in security around key regime buildings and to provide support roles on the front line. Significant numbers of these women (those categorized as 'active' or 'special') received training in using small arms and rocket-propelled grenades (RPGs), but nothing approaching tactical training in infantry warfare.

This member of the Basij is wearing a chemical-warfare suit at the site of a chemical attack by Iraqi forces at Oshnavieh, Iran, on 3 May 1988, although his exposed hands suggest he is likely posing for a staged photograph. (Kaveh Kazemi/ Getty Images)

C

IRANIAN MOBILE TROOPS

(1) Tank commander, 92nd Armoured Division, Operation *Ramadan*, July 1982

The experienced *Gruhban Yekom* (sergeant major) is a long-term professional soldier, his rank denoted by the chevrons on his sleeve (the red outline signifying that he is a member of the armoured branch). He commands an old M47 MBT – a fine vehicle in many ways but not one capable of engaging an Iraqi T-55 or T-62 MBT on equal terms. The backbone of Iran's armoured force was made up of imported British Chieftain Mk 5/3P MBTs, but despite their relative obsolescence tanks such as the M47 (as well as even older examples like the M4 Sherman medium tank) were pressed into service, and suffered losses accordingly. His sidearm is a .45 ACP Colt M1911A1 pistol, an American-made surplus item that came into the Iran along with the purchase of .30-06 M1 Garand rifles and M1 carbines in 1963. The commander wears an AVC (Armoured Vehicle Crewman) DH-132 helmet (featuring an internal liner with radio headset and 'wand' microphone, and covered with a hard ballistic shell), domestically produced tan coveralls and an M56 belt with Israeli yoke.

(2) Mechanized infantryman, 84th *Zafar* Mechanized Brigade IRGC, June 1988

The *Sarbaz Adih* (private of the Revolutionary Guards) is taking part in defending his homeland from Operation *Tawakkalna ala Allah*, one of the late-war hammer-blows delivered by the Iraqis in an attempt to break Iranian resolve once and for all. He wears a domestically produced version of the first-pattern OG-107 utility shirt and trousers with a US-style M56 belt and well-worn boots; and he is taking up a position that will allow him to make the most of his RPG anti-tank rocket launcher when the anticipated columns of Iraqi armour make their approach. He is armed with a Type 69 RPG launcher, a more or less identical Chinese copy of the Soviet RPG-7 that used 85mm HEAT warheads with an effective range of 200m. He carries a pouch for the weapon's sight slung across his shoulder, as well as an old Soviet three-cell pouch on his belt with spare magazines for his 7.62×39mm Type 56-1 assault rifle, the Chinese folding-stock version of the Soviet AKS.

(3) AH-1J Cobra pilot, 1984

The pilot, a *Sotvan Yekom* (first lieutenant) from an Attack Battalion of the 4th General Support Group, has just climbed out of the cockpit of his Bell AH-1J Cobra helicopter gunship after a sortie against Iraqi armour. The AH-1J would prove to be a significant threat to Iraqi armoured forces, despite the fact that nearly all the Iranian-operated fleet lacked the capability to deploy BGM-71 TOW ATGMs. The main weapons were the 20mm M197 triple-barrelled Gatling undernose cannon and 70mm (2.75in) unguided rockets fired from seven- or 19-cell rocket pods carried on stub wings, though as the war progressed the AGM-65A Maverick air-to-ground missile was adapted for use on the AH-1Js which gave a significant boost to their capability. The pilot is wearing a Gentex SPH-4 B Flight Helmet fitted with the Attack Cobra HSS (Helmet Sighting System), a locally produced olive-drab version of the American K2-B flight suit, and aviator-issue Addison flight boots with combined laces and zippers. He carries a US Air Force style survival knife on his belt, as well as a 9×19mm Tariq pistol (an Iraqi licensed and manufactured version of the Italian Beretta M1951) as his sidearm. The Tariq used an eight-round box magazine and was mostly indistinguishable from the Berettas, the exceptions being Arabic lettering on the slide and a marking disc on the grips bearing the likeness of the warrior Tariq ibn Ziyad, famed for leading the Muslim conquest of the Iberian peninsula in the early 8th century.

These Iranian troops are pictured near Ahvaz in April 1982. The soldier in the foreground has hoisted onto his shoulders a 12.7×108mm DShK-type heavy machine gun. The type could be the MGD-12.7, an Iranian licence-produced version of the DShKM; the licence was purchased during the Iran–Iraq War. (Françoise De Mulder/Roger Viollet via Getty Images)

OPPOSITE
Female Basij volunteers receive intensive training in the handling of arms in a camp near Tehran in October 1986. A licensed and locally produced Iranian version of the West German Heckler & Koch G3A3, the G3A6 was an effective and extremely hardwearing rifle, but there weren't enough of them to go around. In the wake of the Islamic Revolution domestic production virtually ceased, not returning to anything like the levels required to keep the IRIA properly equipped for a number of years, forcing the Iranians to rely on captured weapons as well as arms deals with countries such as China and North Korea. (Mohsen Shandiz/Sygma via Getty Images)

Given their ultimate emphasis on supreme sacrifice for the greater good of the regime and for the divine, the Basiji predictably received dreadfully inadequate training, typically lasting just a couple of weeks. Much of their training cycle would be devoted to religious instruction and political indoctrination, delivered by clergy specially selected for their devotion to the regime's core principles. Military-type training was therefore the province of junior officers and NCOs from the IRGC. The short training programme focused on the basics of a mixed infantry/insurgency combat: weapons handling, small-unit offensive and defensive tactics, elementary navigation, night-fighting, infiltration, and so on. The value of the training was limited by many factors, including the short training period allocated, the limited availability and experience of training personnel, and the losses on the front line. As the war dragged on, there was more movement towards incorporating the Basij in larger field training exercises, although this never really bore fruit.

Front-line service

The Basiji stood out through their youth, basic uniforms and weapons, and the red bandannas they tied around their sleeves or heads. They were typically called up for limited tours of duty, usually lasting no more than three months – this was mainly to ensure that they could fulfil their agricultural duties throughout the year – after which they might return home and never again return to the ranks. This might in itself seem to be something approaching a good deal, but they had to survive those three months' service in the first place. The Basiji were renowned for their horrific levels of casualties, especially during periods of major Iranian offensives. It is estimated that more than 155,000 Basiji were 'martyred', with almost one-third of those casualties aged between 15 and 19 and about 3 per cent of casualties below the age of 15. Furthermore, because their period of service could be so short and brutal, those who did survive were of little future military utility.

IRAN'S OTHER PARAMILITARY FORCES

While the IRGC and the Basij constituted Iran's most influential paramilitary forces, the ideological cauldron that was post-revolution Iran spawned and sponsored significant numbers of smaller paramilitary groups, either at a local level or with some pretensions to national status. Many of these are now lost to posterity, but during the Iran–Iraq War some contributed militarily in their own way to the national war effort, either through front-line service or through supporting the Khomeini regime's battle against internal opponents.

The 1987 RAND Corporation report into Iran's paramilitaries identified a number of smaller organizations, including the Sarollah and Ghalollah, tasked with detaining and punishing suspected dissidents and other persons of interest in Iran's cities. The report mentions a subordinate unit, the Khaharan-e Zeynab (Sisters of Zeynab), staffed entirely by women and tasked with policing the populace's ethical conduct. Another organization, the Jondollah, was identified as a close associate of the Gendarmerie (police) forces operating outside the major urban centres, and speculates that it might have been tasked with monitoring the Gendarmerie at the behest of the IRGC (Schahgaldian 1987: 80).

The Gendarmerie actually formed one of Iran's more significant front-line paramilitary units, numbering up to 40,000 members during the conflict. The Imperial Iranian Gendarmerie had been formed back in 1911, and from World War I onwards had something of a tradition of participating in military conflicts as combatants. It survived the Islamic Revolution, putting itself in the service of the new regime, and was principally tasked with counter-insurgency roles in Iranian Kurdistan (Hooten et al. 2018: 32).

The Gendarmerie was organized along military lines, with regiments and battalions, each of the latter consisting of 4–6 companies. For combat roles it formed 'strike units' of company or battalion size. Eventually it had seven regiments and 15 battalions, together constituting a corps. Yet the Gendarmerie was not the most well-supported of units, often armed with outdated and basic equipment; in the battle of Khorramshahr during September–November 1980, for example, its members were seen fighting street battles with bolt-action rifles dating back to World War II.

1 February 1988: Iranian female volunteers, likely serving in the Basij, receive firearms training with Chinese Type 56 rifles at a camp in Tehran; note how their weapons have the folding bayonet swung back in the stored position under the barrel. (Mohsen Shandiz/Sygma via Getty Images)

IRANIAN WEAPONRY AND EQUIPMENT

The equipment and weaponry of the IRIA, and indeed the general ground forces of Iran, reflected the diversity of its pre-war US, British, European and Soviet purchases. The infantry, for example, were mainly armed with the G3A6 battle rifle, an Iranian licence-built version of the West German Heckler & Koch G3A3, with support fire coming from the MGA3 machine gun, another Iranian copy of a West German weapon (it was produced by Iran's Defense Industries Organization), this time the MG1A3, itself a post-war derivative of the MG 42 machine gun.

In terms of armour, Iran had amassed a force of 1,735 main battle tanks (MBTs) by the start of the war. The most prolific type was the British Chieftain Mk 5/3P, of which 875 had been acquired. The rest of the armour mainly consisted of US types, principally the M47, M48 and M60A1 MBTs. Lighter armour consisted of 250 British Scorpion reconnaissance vehicles, *c.*500 Soviet BTR-50, BTR-60 and BTR-152 armoured personnel carriers (APCs), and 325 American M113 APCs. While the Iranian armoured force certainly had a formidable arsenal of MBTs, it suffered severe reliability and maintenance problems with many of its types, especially the Chieftain, which was especially vulnerable to mechanical breakdown in desert conditions; some vehicles required a power pack replacement after fewer than 40 hours of combat use.

Regarding artillery, the Iranians began the war with around 700 major tube artillery pieces, which included a mix of SP and towed types. The former were mainly from American sources – the 175mm M107, 155mm M109 and 203mm M110 – while the latter were a variety of US and Soviet pieces, ranging from 75mm pack howitzers to 203mm M115 howitzers. For anti-tank engagements, the infantry and armoured units could deploy anti-tank guided missiles (ATGMs) supplied by the United States in the form of the BGM-71 TOW (Tube-Launched, Optically Tracked, Wire-Guided) and M47 Dragon, plus the French SS.11, SS.12 and ENTAC. The IRIA also had extensive stocks of air-defence weaponry, with 1,800 anti-aircraft guns in calibres from 20mm to 85mm, 100 Soviet ZSU-23-4 radar-guided quadruple 23mm SP guns, plus extensive stocks of surface-to-air missiles (SAMs) such as the US-supplied HAWK, a medium-range SAM which downed at least 40 Iraqi aircraft during the war.

The aforementioned IRIAA brought a useful rotary fleet to the table. Its major combat and armed assault types were the Agusta-Bell AB.205A and AB.206/206A-1, Bell 214A/C Isfahan and Bell AH-1J Cobra. While the utility and assault types were quite basically armed, usually with 70mm (2.75in) unguided rockets in side-mounted pods and/or a 7.62×51mm General Electric GAU-2B/A electrically powered Minigun, the AH-1J was a pure combat thoroughbred, with an undernose-mounted 20mm M197 triple-barrelled rotary cannon plus stub-wing stores that could include rocket pods and BGM-71 TOW ATGMs. For utility, logistics and further assault roles, helicopter types included the French Aerospatiale SE.316C Alouette III and Soviet Mil Mi-8T and Mi-17 Hips.

Having painted a picture of the very impressive military power of the Iranian ground forces, we must provide a bit more context. As the

An Iranian Marine fires an RPG-7 rocket into an Iraqi position across Arvand Rud (Swift River), also known as the Shatt al-Arab (River of the Arabs), in Abadan, Iran, 1981. The Islamic Republic of Iran Navy provided significant ground forces elements during the Iran–Iraq War, including Marines and Special Forces soldiers, the latter proving especially useful for infiltration operations. (Kaveh Kazemi/ Getty Images)

war went on, skills and spare-parts shortages, plus the endless attrition of combat losses, dramatically reduced the availability and serviceability of major combat equipment. Iran's increasing isolation in the military markets meant that in the later years of the war it had to turn to China and North Korea for low-cost, and generally inferior, alternatives to Soviet equipment. Examples include the YW-531 (Type 63) APC from China; the Chonma-ho I MBT, a North Korean copy of the T-62; and the 240mm M1985 howitzer, also a North Korean import. Yet despite Iraq being the Soviet Union's preferred client, Iran also struck direct military deals with the Soviet Union, estimated to be worth $11.8 billion, for the supply of APCs, 9K11 *Malyutka* (AT-3 Sagger) ATGMs and some numbers of 9K32 *Strela-2* (SA-7 Grail) SAMs. The Kremlin also sold a licence for Iranian manufacture of Soviet small arms, which accounts for the fact that we sometimes see Iranian troops with 7.62mm AK-47 assault rifles rather than the G3A6. Despite US-imposed arms embargoes, the Iranians also received supplies of military hardware from a patchwork of international suppliers, including (with examples of what they provided) Italy

D

IRANIAN SPECIAL FORCES

(1) Paratrooper, 23rd Commando Division, 1985

The paratrooper *Gruhban Dovom* (sergeant) has returned from a heavy engagement, swapping his M62 helmet for his unit's distinctive dark-green beret, a legacy of the training the old brigade underwent with the Americans in the time of the Shah. Originally established in 1959 as the 23rd Special Forces Brigade, the unit evolved through the 1970s thanks to American influence, particularly from the John F. Kennedy Special Warfare Center and School at Fort Bragg, North Carolina. Renamed the 23rd Commando Division after the Islamic Revolution, the unit's paratroopers were certainly among the best-trained forces at the Khomeini regime's disposal. He wears a custom camouflage jacket that seems to have been exclusive to Iranian airborne forces; it was almost certainly of domestic design, probably inspired by French and Israeli styles, and looked to be more robust than the OG-107 copies that dressed the majority of IRIA troops. It also had four patch pockets and used an Iranian variant of the British 1967 DPM design that was a pre-revolutionary signifier of a unit's elite status. The webbing is Israeli-manufactured, the large FAL magazine pouches suitable for the Iranian G3A6 battle rifle that the paratrooper carries. The nature of his duties means that he has been issued with the collapsible-stock version of the G3A6 (the G3A43 in German parlance, though seemingly without a distinct designation in Iran), but despite the reduction in size the weapon still weighed in at a hefty 4.7kg.

(2) Naval Commando, 1st *Takavar* Marine Battalion, Khorramshahr, 1980

The *Takavar* (attack trooper) has been heavily involved in the fight for the blighted city of Khorramshahr, giving as little ground as possible in spite of the desperately unfavourable odds. His squad is conducting a fighting retreat, but as a *Sarjukhe* (corporal) it is his job to maintain cohesion and keep the enemy at bay. He wears a sand-painted M62 helmet, a basic but effective item of head protection, certainly better able to deflect shrapnel and flying debris than the compressed canvas of the Iraqi M80 helmet. The M62 was the third iteration

of US M1-style helmets produced in West Germany, and became the main helmet of the Iranian forces throughout the war, though there were shortages (especially early on in the war) that saw a variety of older models pressed into service as well, particularly among the young and eager recruits of the Pasdaran. His uniform is a domestically produced version of the US OG-107 2nd pattern, but with the shirt made from a 'brushstroke'-pattern camouflage material that was in use by the IRIA's SF units, such as the 23rd Special Forces Brigade (as it then was) and naval special-operations units during the latter period of the Shah's reign, usage that continued into the early years of the Iran–Iraq War. His equipment is of Israeli manufacture, as is his 9×19mm Uzi submachine gun, a number of which came into Iran during the Shah's reign, where they found service with the Naval *Takavaran*.

(3) Naval Commando radioman, 106th *Sajjad* Brigade (IRGC), *Karbala 4*, December 1986

The *Takavar* is a member of Task Force Karbala, serving in one of the IRGC's naval SF brigades. In many ways the IRGC was a direct competitor to the more established Islamic Republic of Iran Navy units, but by this stage of the war there was little doubt as to who was responsible for the direction of events. The *Takavar* is pressed up against one of the numerous earthen berms that dominate the waterlogged terrain of the Shatt al-Arab, peering over the lip while he calls in a report on his radio. He wears a knitted woollen cap, a blue anorak that was common to the IRGC naval brigades, and some rather worn OG-507-style trousers. He wears a *shemagh* scarf (also a very common item among IRGC naval units) for extra warmth, and an Iranian-made version of the Chinese three-cell chest rig. He carries a 7.62×39mm AKMS assault rifle, but his most important tool is the AN/PRC-77 Portable Transceiver that he carries on his back. The American-designed and -manufactured AN/PRC-77 entered US service in 1968, and proved to be an excellent man-portable radio system; it could handle encrypted voice communications, operated in the frequency bands 30.00–52.95MHz (Low Channel) and 53.00–75.95MHz (High Channel), had 920 channels across two bands (using 50kHz steps) and a range of 8km, terrain permitting.

Iranian personnel in vivid blue NBC suits and M17 gas masks participate in the Army Day parade on 18 April 1986, shortly after the unsuccessful Iranian effort to capture the port city of Umm Qasr in southern Iraq. They are armed with G3A6 battle rifles which have their bayonets fitted, the bayonet sitting above the muzzle rather than the more conventional below-muzzle arrangement. (Mohamad ESLAMI RAD/Gamma-Rapho via Getty Images)

(OTO Melara howitzers and land mines), Spain (mortar bombs and recoilless rifles), Greece (engines for M40 and M60 MBTs) and Singapore (Bofors guns and RBS-70 man-portable air-defence systems (MANPADS), as well as contributions from Argentina, Pakistan, Czechoslovakia, Portugal, South Korea and others. There were also unofficial supplies of arms from the United States, via a circuitous back-end sales channel through Israel and private contractors, which gave the Iranians access to weapons such as TOW ATGMs, HAWK SAMs, mortars and howitzer ammunition, and which later saw the United States mired in political scandal.

The IRGC drew on the same equipment as the regular Army. In infantry actions, the G3A6 battle rifle, MGA3 machine gun and RPG were central, with support fire coming from howitzers, MLRS, heavy mortars, ATGMs and SAMs. The Pasdaran became especially adept with the RPG and also the US M47 Dragon ATGM (see Plate B1), a man-portable, shoulder-fired wire-guided weapon that used a SACLOS (semi-automatic command to line of sight) targeting system.

25 May 1988: Basij personnel assemble in gas masks and chemical-warfare suits, during a simulation of a chemical attack at Shahr-e-Rey in the southern suburbs of Tehran. They are wearing what appear to be locally produced decontamination suits and are equipped with the US-made M17 gas mask, which included features such as an inbuilt voice-emitter system and an access tube for drinking from an M1 canteen. The Iran–Iraq War saw one of the last major uses of chemical weapons in modern history, with some individual attacks accounting for up to 8,000 Iranian casualties. Saddam's chemical-warfare teams used both traditional gas weapons such as mustard gas, and advanced nerve agents such as Tabun and Sarin. (Kaveh Kazemi/Getty Images)

Iranian soldiers prepare to fire a heavy mortar on the Allah Akbar front, near Ahvaz, Iran, on 9 December 1980. Mortars were ideal weapons once the war had settled into a fairly static routine, as their high trajectory of fire meant the mortar teams could engage the enemy from deeply dug trenches and gun positions. These soldiers wear a mix of khaki combat and fatigue uniform items plus the M80 compressed-canvas helmet; these particularly helmets have been left in their base green colour, rather than applying the common practice of painting them in desert tan colour. (Kaveh Kazemi/ Getty Images)

THE IRAQI ARMY

Much like Iran, Iraq's military forces were profoundly shaped by political, ideological and personality influences at the very highest levels. For the Iraqis, the key figure was Saddam Hussein Abd al-Majid al-Tikriti, a man known for his paranoid and violent power-play within every aspect of Iraqi society. Following the ascent of the Ba'ath Arab Socialist Party to power in July 1968, with a military coup that overthrew the monarchy, Saddam ruthlessly engineered his path to the top, becoming the Iraqi President in July 1979. The Iraqi Army was especially subject to Saddam's suspicions and control. As President, Saddam conducted his own purge of the military leadership in 1979, removing all corps and divisional commanders and replacing them with Ba'ath loyalists. Again as in Iran, this resulted in the over-promotion of many junior officers and had similar deleterious effects on recruitment and training.

Up to 1979, the Iraqi Army was comparatively weak in relation to Iran. Its defence budget in 1977 was $2.01 billion, a fraction of Iran's $7.9 billion. Furthermore, Iraq had a much smaller population of just 13.5 million, of whom only 1.7 million were eligible for military service.

An Iraqi soldier on the Khorramshahr Front in 1980 takes cover with his Tabuk assault rifle at the ready. The Tabuk was a very basic weapon, without the muzzle compensator of the Soviet AKM and without the chrome-lined bore that helped prevent barrel wear. The maximum effective range of the weapon over iron sights was about 300m. This photograph shows the classic Iraqi Army khaki uniform, plus double-buckle combat boots of a design stretching back to World War II. He has covered his helmet with cloth sacking for basic camouflage. (© Jacques Pavlovsky/Sygma/CORBIS/Sygma via Getty Images)

Nevertheless, Iraq invested heavily in building up its army, the Soviet Union, Czechoslovakia and France being its major suppliers of equipment. By 1979 and the eve of war, Saddam had built up his army to 200,000 men plus 256,000 reservists in 12 divisions and six independent brigades. Saddam also drew upon 80,000 paramilitary warriors, 75,000 in the Iraqi 'Popular Army' alone. Because of the effects of the Islamic Revolution in neighbouring Iran, in 1980 Iraq reached a significant milestone, having achieved numerical superiority in military personnel and operable armour and artillery, which goes a long way to explaining why Saddam chose this year as his moment to strike.

Yet the Iraqi Army had its fair share of issues that compromised operational performance. Despite its lukewarm contribution to the Arab cause in the 1973 Yom Kippur War, the Iraqi Army was mainly configured for internal security and policing duties, with much of its post-1973 combat experience garnered from operations against separatist Kurdish forces in the north of the country. Its training was both heavily politicized and frequently inadequate. Like IRIA, the Iraqi Army had its preferential splits that compromised combined-arms manoeuvres and divisional- and corps-level actions. Saddam's equivalent of the Pasdaran was the Republican Guard, regarded as an elite force of Ba'ath Party loyalists, reporting directly to Saddam himself. The political favour carried by the Republican Guard, plus the need to maintain force levels in the face of casualties of war, led to an impressive expansion of the force during the war years themselves – the Republican Guard had just one armoured brigade in the very first year of the war, but 25 by 1988.

25 September 1980: Iraqi soldiers in buoyant mood during the first days of the Iran–Iraq War. They are wearing a mixture of combat uniforms and fatigues, including at least three colours of beret. Berets were worn by officers, Republican Guard, armoured crews and many other units. (Henri Bureau/Corbis/VCG via Getty Images)

An Iraqi artillery command post coordinates shelling of Abadan and Khorramshahr in October 1980. Both sides in the conflict had made huge investments in the size of their artillery arms prior to the onset of hostilities, fully expecting cross-border bombardments against troop concentrations, cities and major industrial facilities. Iraqi officers – including senior commanders – and men alike were clad in the basic olive-green fatigues being worn here; the berets likely indicate Republican Guard, but they were also worn by several other branches of service. (Bettmann/Getty Images)

Structure and organization

At the beginning of the Iran–Iraq War, the Iraqi Army was divided into three corps, although this number expanded to seven corps (numbered sequentially from I) by the war's end. Each corps had a regionally based headquarters, commanding a combined-arms mix of armoured divisions, infantry divisions and independent support brigades. Eventually the Army would total five armoured divisions, two mechanized divisions and 33 infantry brigades.

An example of corps structure gives an insight into the typical arrangement. III Corps was headquartered in al-Qurnah and located in the sector between Dezful and Abadan. In 1982, it consisted of three armoured

Pictured on 28 February 1984, these Iraqi troops are dressed in a variety of clothing and headgear, including some civilian items. Note the chest rig and binoculars worn by the man in the centre, and the folding-stock Tabuk assault rifles. (François LOCHON/Gamma-Rapho via Getty Images)

divisions (3rd, HQ Tikrit; 6th, HQ Baqubah; and 9th, HQ Samayah), one mechanized division (the 5th, HQ Basrah) and one infantry division (the 11th, HQ Sulaimaniyah), plus 10th Armoured Brigade and 33rd SF Brigade in reserve (Hooten et al. 2019: 12). The number and designations of subordinate brigades per division varied substantially, with the 3rd and 9th Armoured divisions fielding only four apiece, but the 11th Infantry Division no fewer than eight.

Support elements within a corps might include artillery and air defence at brigade strength, and reconnaissance, engineering, bridging, signals and chemical-defence units at battalion strength. An Army mechanized infantry brigade would have an organization of three battalions of infantry (each with up to 50 IFVs/APCs), each battalion of three companies, plus an armoured battalion of about 44 tanks (three companies), a 120mm mortar company and supply, commando, engineer and NBC defence companies. An infantry brigade would have three rifle companies, with three platoons per company and three squads (ten men each) per platoon, plus supply, commando and NBC units at company or platoon strength.

The army corps also had the support of four wings of the Iraqi Army Aviation Corps (IrAAC): 1st Wing (Kirkuk), 2nd Wing (Taji), 3rd Wing (Basra), 4th Wing (Amara). Each wing would typically act in the support of a pair of corps. For example, the 1st Wing supported I and V Corps while the 3rd Wing supported III and VII Corps. Each wing was divided into six attack squadrons, four reconnaissance squadrons, one heavy transport squadron and two light strike squadrons (Hooten et al. 2018: 37).

ABOVE LEFT
Iraqi soldiers show themselves in victorious mood during the offensive operations of 1980, when they made successful incursions across the Shatt al-Arab into Iran. The officer at the front is wearing a uniform in the 'ragged leaf', a traditional Iraqi Army pattern that was generally issued to airborne and commando troops. Note also the single leather AK magazine pouches of the soldier front right; these are probably locally produced. (Alain MINGAM/Gamma-Rapho via Getty Images)

ABOVE RIGHT
25 September 1980: three Iraqi soldiers pose during the opening days of the conflict at Ahvaz, Iran. While the soldier front right has the standard Iraqi eagle badge on his beret, the man on the left has the badge of the transport service. (Henri Bureau/Corbis/VCG via Getty Images)

Recruitment and training

Iraqi society during the 1970s, especially following the 1973 Yom Kippur War and the struggles with Iran and Kurdistan in 1974–75, was increasingly militarized. All Ba'ath Party members aged 18–45, for example, were committed to six hours of military training each week, although the quality of that training could be indifferent, and the degree to which it was taken seriously varied. But for the conventional Iraqi Army, militarization and conscription brought with them respectable strength – 200,000 regular troops and 256,000 reservists at the start of war in 1980. By 1987, however, the Iraqi armed services had 1.7 million men in uniform, the Army accounting for 875,000 (including 480,000 reservists). While sounding

E **IRAQI ARMY INFANTRY**

(1) Grenadier, 41st Infantry Division, 1983

The grenadier stands at the ready, his 7.62×39mm Tabuk assault rifle (a copy of the Yugoslavian Zastava M70B1) fitted with a FAZ anti-tank grenade. He wears an M80 helmet covered with a surplus West German net that was quite distinctive and commonly seen throughout the war. The South Korean M80 helmet itself was made from compressed canvas, and quickly became the main helmet of the Iraqi Army during the war, gradually supplanting the earlier (and substantially more robust) Polish wz. 50 and Soviet-style SSh-40 and SSh-60 models that had previously predominated. His webbing is an imported Pakistani-made version of British Pattern 58 webbing, including the FAL magazine pouches, despite the fact that he carries a Tabuk. Like the original M70B1 the Iraqi version could be quickly identified by the three cooling vents on each side of the wooden handguard, as well as by its grenade-launcher sight that was built over the rifle's gas block which, when raised, stopped the gas system from cycling; the user would swap out the muzzle nut or brake for a spigot adapter (22mm in diameter) over which the rifle grenade would be fitted, and then load and fire a blank cartridge to launch the projectile. The Iraqi rifle grenade appears to be a straight copy of the Yugoslavian M60, an anti-tank shaped-charge projectile capable of penetrating 200mm of armour at a maximum range of 150m. A Yugoslavian anti-personnel fragmentation rifle grenade also existed, the M60P1 (240m maximum range), and it is likely that it (or an Iraqi copy thereof) also saw service in the war.

(2) Light-machine-gunner, 2nd Infantry Division, Khorramshahr, October 1980

The wear of fighting in such a difficult and increasingly inhospitable place has taken its toll on this soldier from the 2nd Infantry Division, who moves forward hesitantly, preparing to round yet another corner in the city that was becoming known as *Khuninshahr*, the 'city of blood'. He wears an old SSh-60 steel helmet roughly overpainted in desert tan, and an Iraqi-made version of a West German parka with a removable fleece lining, an excellent and warming piece of clothing that was much-valued in the often-bitter winter months. His weapon is an Egyptian-made 7.62×39mm RPD (*Ruchnoy Pulemyot Degtyaryova*; Degtyaryov's hand-held machine gun), a squad support weapon that laid down 650rd/min, fed by a 100-round belt that was contained in a carrying drum suspended below the gun. Although the RPD was past its prime, having been superseded by the RPK in

Soviet use, it was a common weapon on the battlefields of the Iran–Iraq War, and a robust and trustworthy one as well.

(3) Marksman, 19th Infantry Division, al-Faw, 1985

An Iraqi marksman makes his way through difficult ground in search of a good spot in which to settle and wait for his targets to come to him. He wears a plain M80 helmet only distinguished by the homemade marking he has applied to the brow; and a locally made British-style military jumper over a DPM shirt and trousers derived from the British 1968 combat uniform. The Iraqi Army's strong historical links to the British armed forces were evident in the Iraqi uniforms and personal equipment by the time of the Iran–Iraq War, not least in the standard infantry khaki shirt, trousers, web belt, gaiters and black boots. The Iraqi Army also wore copies of post-war British DPM uniforms, including combat uniforms and paratrooper smocks. The British influence manifested itself in other ways in the Iraqi Army, notably regimental insignia. The Iraqis also used copies of the British Pattern 44 and Pattern 58 webbing, although these were frequently produced, with variable quality, in Pakistan. This man, though, wears a Chinese-made Type 56 chest rig and is armed with a 7.62×39mm Tabuk Sniper Rifle, which much like the basic Tabuk was copy of a Yugoslavian weapon, in this case the 7.62×39mm Zastava M72B1 light machine gun. The Iraqi version removed the fully automatic fire option of the M72B1, and was thus also able to utilize a much lighter barrel and dispense with the bipod, but the receiver remained essentially unchanged; and the Tabuk Sniper Rifle could use the same 30-round box magazines as a standard AKM-style assault rifle, though 10-, 15- and 20-round versions were also available to aid in firing when prone. Despite its superficially similar appearance to the Soviet 7.62×54mmR SVD-63 (as well as the Romanian 7.62×54mmR PIL and Yugoslavian 7.92×57mm Zastava M76), and the fact that it was meant to allow its user to fulfil a similar role – that of a designated marksman, hitting enemies at ranges beyond those achievable by assault rifles – the Tabuk Sniper Rifle was dissimilar in several important ways, the most significant of which was the fact that it was chambered for the 7.62×39mm intermediate cartridge. The 600mm barrel allowed for hits at greater range and with better accuracy than the AKM, but it was unable to compete with the SVD-63's, PIL's or M76's full-power cartridges in either range or stopping power. The Tabuk Sniper Rifle could mount optics using the side-bracket system common to AK-platform weapons, often the Romanian 4× LPS scope or as with this example, a Soviet 4× PSO-1 sight.

impressive, these bare figures mask the fact that the Iraqi Army was plagued by manpower shortages on the front lines, with almost all divisions and brigades significantly understrength. For this reason, Army soldiers might find themselves doing multiple front-line tours over the duration of the war. The conscription period was officially 20–21 months, but between 1980 and 1988 it was frequently longer, increasing the likelihood of the soldier becoming a casualty statistic.

The conscription efforts overwhelmingly focused upon poor and illiterate young men, mainly of Shi'ite faith but generally under the leadership of Sunni officers (reflecting the minority faith of the country's leadership), especially those from Tikrit and Mosul. Only later in the war did the conscription pool widen to include some of those higher ranks of society; from 1986 some 125,000 university lecturers and students were conscripted, having previously been exempt. (Hooten et al. 2018: 35). The recruiting effort had a strong element of compulsion about it, the regime frequently combing the major cities for new recruits, often extracting multiple eligible sons from the same family.

The sources are unclear regarding the period and extent of basic training, but it was clear that it was inadequate on several levels, especially at the beginning of the war and also in terms of technical training. This was not just an issue of widespread illiteracy it shared with Iran. As we shall see, the Iraqi armed forces acquired a bewildering spectrum of foreign weapons and equipment during the 1970s but often without the corresponding transfer of tactical or technical expertise. Despite the presence of some 1,200 foreign trainers and advisors in-country, the result was a lack of high-level insight. This being said, as the war progressed Saddam's regime did make conscious efforts to improve the professionalism and competence of the Army, although

much of this focus was on the officers. He eventually allowed non-Ba'athists to enter the military academies and to take mid-level commands. Among the rank and file, however, morale was low and the level of desertion was high (possibly as high as 5 per cent), and both were exacerbated by the continual effects of high combat losses.

Front-line service

The physical conditions for Iraqi troops on the front line were marginally better than those for Iranian forces, especially in terms of food and basic supplies, on account of the better Iraqi logistics described above (aided by the fact that Iraq is also a much smaller country than neighbouring Iran). This being said, they still faced the same heat and dust as the Iranians, which had severe effects on men and maintenance.

In one sense, Iraq's access to the broader international arms market created as many problems as it solved. A key problem for front-line troops, especially those in armoured, mechanized and specialist support units, was the frequent introduction of new equipment and weapon types. Without the full training infrastructure for the fresh piece of kit, and the time available to acclimatize to it before going into combat, many pieces of equipment were used with less-than-optimal efficiency. Those individuals who did have the skills, literacy and knowledge required to use a piece of equipment might find themselves regularly rotated out to other units, thereby depriving their home unit of the continuity of their technical expertise. The situation also meant that units might find themselves operating many different types of weapons, thus preventing units from having the standardization most conducive to efficient coordination between forces.

ABOVE LEFT
Two Iraqi soldiers are pictured on 22 March 1985, during the battle for the al-Howeizah marshes, north of Basra. The soldier on the right appears to have a British-style M58 ammunition pouch, a type common in Iraqi service. (JEAN-CLAUDE DELMAS/AFP via Getty Images)

ABOVE RIGHT
An Iraqi infantryman guarding his post, 1987. This image shows the typical Iraqi combat uniform and equipment of this period, including the M80 helmet, a West German-issue military parka, and the distinctive Chinese Type 56 chest rig for his small-arms ammunition and other pieces of kit, such as first-aid packs. (Thomas Hartwell/The LIFE Images Collection via Getty Images/Getty Images)

Pictured during a training exercise on 19 October 1983, this mud-caked Iraqi soldier wears a helmet with painted camouflage and is armed with a Tabuk assault rifle. His uniform's camouflage is in a 'brushstroke' pattern influenced by British camouflage designs of the 1950s. (Pierre PERRIN/ Gamma-Rapho via Getty Images)

For long periods of the Iran–Iraq War, Iraq was operating under a particularly defensive mind set, holding the lines around its borders against regular Iranian offensives. This was not a matter of over-caution; the sheer size of Iran, the location of Tehran nearly 800km east of the Iran–Iraq border and the limitations of Iraqi manpower meant that there was no possibility of Iraqi forces making deep offensive incursions into Iran, at least not ones that would adequately threaten or destabilize the Khomeini regime. The Iraqi soldiers deployed to these border positions faced perilous days, with regular poundings from Iranian artillery, punctuated by whirling and terrifying Iranian infantry assaults, which had to be held back with

heavy firepower. The Iraqi forces did make defensive innovations, however. For example, they increased the volume of minefield defences on a massive scale; Lieutenant General Ra'ad al-Hamdani, a former Iraqi Republican Guard II Corps commander, remembered that the volume of mines was increased 'tenfold', with mine coverage at one mine (both anti-personnel and anti-armour) every metre over hundreds of square metres, thus ensuring that no-one could pass through successfully, hence the Iranian use of brutal human-wave mine-clearing operations (Woods et al. 2009: 46). Iraqi forces also diversified their defensive activities in an attempt to stop Iranian infiltration actions, increasing the volumes of patrols by both regular infantry and SF in an attempt to spot infiltration actions at the moment of inception.

Iraqi armour had more of a focus on mass and firepower than on fire and manoeuvre. The armoured force was something of a strange hybrid: heavily equipped with Soviet-style weapons and equipment but without acquiring much of Soviet combat doctrine; thrown into a major conventional war but more historically practiced in internal policing and counter-insurgency. In situations requiring creative and offensive thinking, such as urban warfare, the Iraqi Army relied heavily upon its SF units to generate tactical dynamism. This resulted in the overuse of such men, so much so that by the end of 1982 their ranks were critically depleted and had to be rebuilt over the following years. In the end, however, the Iraqi Army demonstrated that in defence of its homeland it could be tenacious, and when it did finally go back on the offensive it did so against significantly weakened Iranian armed forces.

20 April 1988: Iraqi soldiers celebrate their victory over Iran in the strategic al-Faw Peninsula in south-east Iraq. On 17 April 1988 some 100,000 Iraqi troops, roughly 60 per cent of them from the Republican Guard, mounted a rapid operation to seize the peninsula back from the Iranians, who had occupied it for the previous two years. The fighting included the widespread use of chemical weapons by the Iraqis and was timed to coincide with a major US strike on Iranian naval assets, codenamed Operation *Praying Mantis*. (MIKE NELSON/ AFP via Getty Images)

THE IRAQI REPUBLICAN GUARD

The *Haras al-Iraq al-Jamhuri* (Iraqi Republican Guard) largely came to prominence in the West during the 1991 Gulf War, when the Western media first feared the presence then celebrated the defeat of Republican Guard formations in the battle to liberate Kuwait. Yet the Republican Guard had a long ancestry by this point in history, having been formed in 1963 through the conversion of the Iraqi Army's 20th Brigade into a force ideologically dedicated to supporting the then-new revolutionary Ba'ath Arab Socialist Party. The role of the Republican Guard was initially to act as a sort of bodyguard force, shielding the Baghdad regime from internal enemies, including threats from the conventional military. Over time, and especially once its loyalty was switched to Saddam Hussein, it became the sizeable elite of the Iraqi armed forces, at the vanguard of Saddam's final victories in

F | IRAQI REPUBLICAN GUARD TROOPS

(1) Radioman, 1st Republican Guard Mechanized Brigade, 1983

This Guardsman's simple uniform sports the relatively common 'waves'-pattern camouflage used throughout the war; the uniforms were manufactured in and imported from Jordan, though the pattern originally came from South Korea where it was intended for use by that country's special forces. As a general rule, camouflage uniforms were mainly the preserve of Iraqi airborne, commando and other SF units, the camouflage acting as a visible display of elite status, although items might gravitate outwards into other units. Like the Iranians, the Iraqis wore the 'brushstroke'-pattern camouflage, drawing on Belgian and West German patterns. Some Iraqi ground troops wore West German M1955 Bundeswehr combat uniforms, with a vertical-stripe design, while others can be seen in French 'lizard'-pattern camouflage. It has also been observed that in the mid- to late 1980s Iraqi soldiers (mainly in the Popular Army and the Republican Guard) occasionally used the US Army's M1948 Engineer Research and Development Laboratory (ERDL) leaf-pattern camouflage. This man's M80 helmet is clearly home-painted in an attempt at concealment. His British Pattern 44 webbing and pack are Pakistani-made, and his PRC-439 radio was made in Italy by IRET specifically for export, as it was deemed of unsuitable quality for the Italian armed forces. Its light weight (just 4kg) and small size made it a good choice as a tactical radio to equip combat troops, the VHF/FM transceiver having a frequency range of 40–50MHz.

(2) PK machine-gunner, *Medina* Division, 1982

The *Jundi* (private) has taken the precaution of pulling on his gas mask in case of blowback from the chemical attack currently under way to soften up the Iranian positions before the 'push' begins. A distinguishing insignia of the Republican Guard was a red-coloured cloth triangle worn on each shoulder, occasionally edged in white. Although far from universally worn, a red shoulder lanyard was another Republican Guard distinction (see page 51). Iraqi Army and Republican Guard troops might be seen wearing black berets, these being badged with gilt, bronze, black or grey eagle badges, representing the Iraqi coat of arms. Republican Guard troops might also have a scarlet ribbon sewn onto the cap by the side of the badge, to denote their commitment to the regime of Saddam Hussein and/or their bravery in combat. This man wears a sand-coloured M80 helmet with hand-painted Republican Guard markings in red, a dark-green uniform marked on both shoulders with the red triangle of the Republican Guard (the bar under his right shoulder insignia is a mark of his rank), and British-style ankle boots. His webbing is an Iraqi-made version of British Pattern 44 items (a belt, yoke and pouches), but his most important piece of equipment is his gas mask, an export version of the Yugoslavian M1 that was developed in the 1960s, and would see plenty of use (along with many other varieties) in the war. It often came with an LPD kit (*Licni Pribor za Dekontaminaciju*; personal decontamination kit) in the bag, with Iraqi examples being marked up in Arabic. His weapon, the PK (*Pulemyot Kalashnikova*; Kalashnikov's machine gun), was an outstandingly good general-purpose machine gun in the right hands. He will rely on the bipod when using the PK in its light-machine-gun role, laying down fire at 650rd/min out to ranges of 1,000m (up to a maximum of 3,800m when mounted on a tripod).

(3) Major, Republican Guard, 1985

The *Ra 'Ed* (major) is taking part in a live-fire training exercise for new recruits to his division. He wears a black beret with a golden Iraqi eagle pin, a sign of elite status, and a camouflage uniform in the 'vertical stripe' pattern, a locally produced variation on the West German M1955 Bundeswehr combat uniform design that had been imported by Iraq (and a number of other countries). His belt and holster are Pakistani-made versions of British Pattern 58 equipment. His assault rifle is a 7.62×39mm PM md. 63, a Romanian version of the much-copied Soviet AKM and readily identifiable by its shaped wooden pistol foregrip. He also carries a 9×19mm CZ-75 pistol in his holster (originally designed for a Browning Hi-Power, but easily able to accommodate the Czech weapon); the CZ-75 was one of the new generation of 9mm pistols with staggered magazines that allowed for greater capacity (12 rounds in the detachable box magazine, in the case of the CZ), and proved to be a reliable and popular handgun. It was not an issue weapon for the Iraqi Popular Army or Republican Guard, however, making this a privately obtained example – a common practice among Iraqi officers.

the Iran–Iraq War. The regular Iraqi Army would become ever more aware that it was playing second fiddle to this well-supported and materially privileged force.

Structure and organization

At the beginning of the Iran–Iraq War, the Iraqi Republican Guard consisted of just the al-Haris al-Jamhuri (Republican Guard Brigade) of four battalions, supplemented by some men from the 31st Special Forces Brigade and operating under the authority of II Corps. The growth of the Republican Guard began moderately at the beginning of 1986, when a Republican Guard Armoured Division was formed, consisting of the 3rd Republican Guard Special Forces Brigade and the 4th Republican Guard Infantry Brigade. These were just the first steps in a huge programme of expansion, however, as Saddam sought to create an elite vanguard that would ultimately be able to break the deadlock war on the borders. By the end of 1986, four divisions had been created, with a total of 11 brigades, and by 1988 the Republican Guard would reach its maximum size and strength of ten divisions with 25 brigades and a total manpower of 103,000 men, all consolidated into the Republican Guard Forces Command, a corps-level formation. This formation was fundamentally part of the Iraqi Army structure, although it still directed its primary loyalty towards Saddam Hussein as its ultimate chief (its actual commander was General Hussein Rashid Wandawi al-Tikriti, the General Staff's Deputy Chief of Staff for Operations, although he reported directly to Saddam).

The Republican Guard corps was a mix of armoured, infantry and SF formations. The prestige of these formations was not only evoked by the

Iraqi troops conduct assault training in October 1983. The red lanyard (*qardoon*) running through the shoulder strap on the right shoulder was a distinguishing feature of Republican Guard uniform, although not always worn. (Pierre PERRIN/Gamma-Rapho via Getty Images)

Republican Guard label, but also, in the case of some, through the cultural references of their honorifics. The 1st *Hammurabi* Armoured Division, for example, was named after Hammurabi (r. *c*.1792–*c*.1750 BC), the Babylonian king who laid down the legal framework called the Code of Hammurabi, one of history's earliest surviving codes of law. The *Nebuchadnezzar* Motorized Division, meanwhile, was named after Nebuchadnezzar II (r. *c*.605–562 BC), the second king of the Neo-Babylonian Empire.

The order of battle for the Republican Guard during the Iran–Iraq War is very confused and contradictory in modern reference sources, making it difficult to be definitive. This lack of clarity is likely due to the flexibility of organization inherent within the Republican Guard itself during this period, with units changing their internal composition to reflect operational realities and combat movements, divisions expanding and contracting with the addition or subtraction of supporting brigades. A typical order of battle for a Republican Guard armoured division might be as follows. The armoured element would be provided by two tank brigades, each of three tank battalions, with each of the brigades also containing a mechanized infantry battalion, an engineering company, a motorized SF company, a reconnaissance platoon and a rocket-launcher battery. There would also be a mechanized infantry brigade, again with three battalions, plus a tank battalion, anti-armour company, and much the same support units as in the two tank brigades. A divisional artillery brigade would deliver the heavy long-range firepower, typically through seven SP battalions of 122mm, 152mm and 155mm howitzers. Rounding off the four-brigade structure might be additional SF battalions and reconnaissance, anti-tank and engineer battalions. Overall, Republican Guard divisions were larger and more powerful than their Iraqi Army equivalents – another factor reflecting the greater status of the formation.

At least two styles of camouflage clothing are evident in this photograph from October 1983 depicting Iraqi troops in training. There are also two different helmet types on display: most of the soldiers are wearing the compressed-canvas M80, which features a flared rim, while the soldier to the right and in the foreground seems to be wearing an SSh-60, or similar Soviet-style helmet. (Pierre PERRIN/Gamma-Rapho via Getty Images)

This photograph of Iraqi troops in training on 19 October 1983 offers a clear view of one of the many camouflage patterns worn during the war with Iran. This particular pattern appears inspired by 1950s and 1960s West German patterns. (Pierre PERRIN/Gamma-Rapho via Getty Images)

Recruitment and training

Republican Guard recruitment policies were highly selective, to ensure the political and ethnic loyalty to Saddam and the Ba'ath Party regime. For the first years of Saddam's reign, and of the Iran–Iraq War, the main recruiting pool was Sunni Arabs and loyal Ba'athists from the area north of Baghdad. High numbers of recruits, especially those filling out the officer ranks, came directly from Saddam's own home town of Tikrit and his al-Begat tribal group, in turn a sub-group of the Al-Bu Nasir tribe.

Because of its elite status, and because it was answerable directly to Saddam as its commander-in-chief (high-ranking officer nominations would often come straight from Saddam himself), the Republican Guard had recruiters who could be far more selective and elitist in their recruit acquisitions. They also fostered the migration of high-performing talent in the regular Army across to the Republican Guard. The task of recruitment was made that much easier by the fact that those in the Republican Guard received higher salaries and better conditions of service, plus a certain cachet, compared to those in the regular Army.

A seismic shift in the recruitment and training of the Republican Guards came in 1986, when the Republican Guard began a mighty growth in size, prompted by Saddam's need to create a more offensive and capable army and to patch up gaps in front-line manpower caused by combat losses. The basket of manpower eligible for Republican Guard service was significantly widened, moving away from an emphasis on a localized all-volunteer to incorporate a far wider swathe of potential recruits between 17 and 41 years of age. In addition to a conscription programme, a major source of new manpower was further transfers from the regular Army, particularly experienced and battle-proven officers, who were often used to form the core of HQ staff for a new formation. There was also the temporary assignment of entire Army battalions and brigades to establish the framework for a new division (Hooten et al. 2018: 39). Now there was no longer the need to be a demonstrative Ba'ath Party member, although being such was still an important criterion for promotion and advancement through the ranks. The recruitment drive also widened its focus to include the professional and educated classes, especially university students.

Another long-standing benefit of being in the Republican Guard was that recruits would generally receive a far higher standard of training compared to that of other ground forces units, in turn reinforced by access to the best equipment on offer. The expansion period of the Republican Guard from 1986 resulted in further investment to improve training standards. The trainers were partly from within the Republican Guard, but the scale and pace of the expansion meant that they were not sufficient in number, thus Republican Guard units were often trained by some of the best Army instructors and by pairing Republican Guard units with regular Army equivalents. The major training area for the Republican Guard was the al-Habbaniyah site (formerly Royal Air Force

19 October 1983: Iraqi troops practise bayonet fighting. Given their camouflage uniforms, which were generally reserved for more elite units, they are likely to be soldiers of the Republican Guard. The camouflage itself is one several 'brushstroke' patterns worn by Iraq during this period, with British, West German, French and Belgian influences. (Pierre PERRIN/Gamma-Rapho via Getty Images)

Station Habbaniya) in al-Anbar province, just to the west of Baghdad. It was a vast training area and base – in its RAF days it had housed 10,000 people – and it included facilities such as swimming pools, mosques and cinemas. It was also the site for the production of Iraqi mustard gas weapons. The base was large enough for the Republican Guard to conduct divisional-level combined-arms exercises, helping the force to develop the more offensive mind set that was required if Iraq was to turn the tide against Iran late in the war.

The elite status of the Republican Guard, and the benefits that brought with it, generated a higher sense of morale among its units than among many other Iraqi land forces. Yet we should not take this line of reasoning too far, because with favourable status came responsibility. Lieutenant General Ra'ad al-Hamdani noted in an interview after the war that many officers in the Iraqi Army were actually reluctant to transfer to the Republican Guard because of the requirement to accept the responsibility that came with 'high-level missions, and high levels of expectations and sacrifices', plus up to '365 days' of training (Woods et al. 2009: 60).

G IRAQI MOBILE TROOPS

(1) Tank commander, 8th Armoured Brigade, *Hammurabi* Armoured Division, 1982

This commander of a T-62 MBT has just baled out of his destroyed tank and drawn his sidearm to defend himself. The *Mulazim* (second lieutenant) wears olive-drab overalls, made notable by Republican Guard insignia in the form of a red triangular patch on each shoulder and the red lanyard hanging from his right shoulder; his rank is denoted by the single star on his shoulder slides. Tank crews wore coveralls in a variety of designs and colours, including Soviet-style black suits as well as locally produced tan and khaki varieties, not to mention ordinary uniforms. The tank commander is armed with an M84 machine pistol, the Yugoslavian-licensed version of the Czechoslovakian Skorpion vz. 61, as his personal defence weapon. The Skorpion was a machine pistol specifically designed for second-line personnel, vehicle crews and other soldiers who required a weapon more substantial than a pistol but who didn't need (or didn't have the space for) a full-sized infantry rifle. Capable of fully automatic fire, the Skorpion was chambered for the .32 ACP (7.65×17mm Browning SR) cartridge and could use 10- or 20-round box magazines (the 10-round magazine was usually fitted in the weapon when holstered, with two spare 20-round magazines carried in a belt pouch).

(2) Mechanized infantryman, 1st Mechanized Division, 1982

The *Na'ib 'arif*'s (corporal's) squad has just debouched from its Czech-built OT-64A SKOT (*Stredni Kolovy Obrneny Transporter*; medium wheeled armoured transporter) during the early stages of Operation *Ramadan*, also known as the First Battle of al-Basrah, which took place from 13 July to 3 August 1982. He wears a Polish wz. 50 helmet covered in burlap and a rather ragged green nylon helmet net, also from Poland. His tan uniform is roughly made but serviceable; his chest rig is a domestically made version of the Chinese Type 56 style, with room for three magazines as well as F1-type hand grenades or other sundries. He is armed with a Yugoslavian-made 7.62×39mm Zastava M70AB2 assault rifle

(the 'A' representing the fact that it is the version with an underfolding stock). The most obvious distinguishing feature on the Zastava was the three cooling vents on each side of the rifle's wooden handguard, as opposed to two for other AK-type assault rifles, a characteristic that would be carried over on the Iraqi Tabuk. The M70 series was yet another Eastern Bloc variant on the Soviet AKM assault rifle, though one that was reverse-engineered rather than being an official derivative (the political distance between Yugoslavia and the Soviet Union, including the former's refusal to join the Warsaw Pact, meant that the Yugoslavs didn't receive the AK-47 or AKM technical package). Although M70 assault rifles were more or less identical in capability and performance to other AKMs (coming in both fixed- and folding-stock versions), they had one unusual feature – an in-built capacity to fire rifle grenades. This required a thicker-stamped receiver (1.5mm as opposed to the AKM's 1mm), a different latch for the top cover to ensure it wouldn't be jarred loose by the discharge of a grenade, and a permanent sight bracket over the gas block that shut off the gas system when it was raised.

(3) Mil Mi-25 pilot, No. 66 Squadron, 1985

The pilot is readying himself for a sortie against Iranian forces in late 1985. He flies the Mil Mi-25 helicopter gunship, the export version of the Mi-24 Hind that had acquired such a fearsome reputation in the wake of the Soviet Union's invasion of Afghanistan in 1979. Iraq acquired at least two dozen Mi-25s between 1980 and 1985, and they proved to be highly capable machines able to engage both Iranian ground targets and helicopters. Aside from its 12.7mm Yakushev-Borzov Yak-B four-barrelled undernose rotary cannon, the Mi-25 could carry 9M17P *Falanga* (AT-2 Swatter) anti-tank missiles and 57mm UB-32 rockets in reusable 32-salvo pods affixed to the hardpoints of its stub wings. Iraqi Mi-25 pilots were Soviet-trained, and a degree of their equipment was also from the same source; the pilot wears a ZSh-3B flight helmet and a HAS-N survival vest over Soviet-issue coveralls, and carries a 9×18mm Makarov pistol as his sidearm.

The Iraqi dictator Saddam Hussein visits the front line with members of his staff, July 1987. He wears a simple British-pattern khaki service-dress uniform with major-general rank indicated on his shoulder boards. He also wears the red lanyard of the Republican Guard. (Jacques Pavlovsky/Sygma via Getty Images)

Front-line service

The expansion and increasing professionalization of the Republican Guard was one of the deciding factors that tilted the war in Saddam's favour between 1986 and 1988. What the Republican Guard brought to the table was both an offensive spirit and the tactical proficiency to turn that spirit into meaningful action. They could deliver major attacks with an improved capability in combined-arms coordination, particularly between mechanized infantry, armour, rotary-wing aviation, and artillery, and they demonstrated that they could work comfortably alongside regular Army formations. Through these skills, the Republican Guard returned the tactical dominance to Iraq in 1987 and 1988, something it had not possessed since the early 1980s.

A good example of the Republican Guard in action was their role in clearing Iranian forces out of the al-Faw Peninsula in April 1987. With the Iraqi Army's 6th Armoured and 7th Infantry divisions attacking the peninsula from the north, the Republican Guard's *Madina Al-Munawara* and *Hammurabi* Armoured divisions and the *Baghdad* Infantry Division assaulted from the south. Such was the violent momentum of this push, and the confidence with which it was delivered, that within just 35 hours the peninsula was back in Iraqi hands, despite the fact that five days had been deemed as realistic for such an outcome.

The Republican Guard was not only capable when on the attack, however; it could also manage a defence, as many Iranian units found to their cost in ill-conceived frontal attacks during the later years of the war. Furthermore, the Republican Guard showed that it was capable of tactical turnarounds, reversing tactical retreats in short order and taking back any Iranian gains. It was for such reasons that the Republican Guard was so feared by the Coalition during the subsequent 1991 Gulf War, although in that conflict the technological and tactical superiority of the Coalition forces (especially in terms of airpower and surveillance) meant that the Republican Guard was simply outclassed on the battlefield.

IRAQI PARAMILITARY FORCES

Iraq utilized paramilitary forces as much as Iran during the Iran–Iraq War, although often without the ideological fervour or political reliability that characterized the Pasdaran and the Basij.

The Iraqi Border Guard

The smallest of its paramilitary elements was the Iraqi Border Guard, which was essentially a border police force with light-infantry training. On paper its strength reached a peak of 24 brigades, but in reality only about 5,000 of its men served in combat duties during the Iran–Iraq War, after the Border Guard was transferred to Army authority in February 1980. It was principally used in counter-insurgency roles against internal enemies.

The Popular Army

The Iraqi Popular Army, also known as the People's Army, can be viewed as an Iraqi version of the Pasdaran, being a militarized civilian volunteer force dedicated to protecting and preserving the Baghdad regime, and providing a counter-balancing force to the regular Army. It was formed in February 1970, the recruitment focusing on men (and some women) aged 18 and over who were politically reliable Ba'ath Party members (although this rule was not always enforced) and who had ideally completed military service or training. From 1986, with Saddam looking to bulk out its manpower, the recruitment umbrella for the Popular Army was opened further to incorporate men up to the age of 42, and schools and universities were combed for recruits. In the very last year of the war, however, a definite element of moral coercion was introduced into the otherwise voluntary nature of service in the Popular Army. Ba'ath Party recruiters and local communities placed pressure on individuals and families to offer up Popular Army recruits, and there was even some threat of punishment for those who resisted doing so, such as the withdrawal of ration cards.

As explained in previous sections, Ba'ath Party members would acquire some basic military training, and the Popular Army members attended two-months of further training at special camps throughout the year. The nature and quality of the training was haphazard, but tended to focus on basic weapons handling, small-unit manoeuvres, position assaults, search operations and even, for the Popular Army's troops designated as 'commandos', air-assault tactics.

An Iraqi soldier stands in the swamp near the Iraqi city of al-Howeizah, north of Basra, on 20 March 1985. Note the helmet netting; Iraqi troops also used helmet coverings of sand-coloured cloth. (JEAN-CLAUDE DELMAS/AFP via Getty Images)

As soldiers, however, the men turned out by the training regimes were of highly variable quality. Nevertheless, it was a productive process – at its peak in the late-war years, the Popular Army numbered some 250,000 personnel.

Organizationally, the Popular Army was structured around 19 divisions arranged regionally, with a GHQ in Baghdad and district HQs in each of the 18 administrative provinces. Each of the provinces was separated into sectors, and each of the sectors was divided in turn into ten 'bases'. The bases were designated according to type: command bases; infantry/combat bases; support bases (light mortars and machine guns); and anti-aircraft bases. Despite the ostensible military coherence of this structure, however, the Popular Army was a crude and blunt instrument in war. It could

H IRAQI SPECIAL FORCES

(1) Guardsman, 11 Commando Brigade (Republican Guard), 1984

The Guardsman wears the black beret customary among Republican Guard units (particularly their SF units), a tan shirt with Republican Guard insignia on the shoulders, and camouflage trousers in the 'blue brushstroke' pattern, originally a Belgian design that was adapted for manufacture and export in West Germany. Mismatched items of clothing, both at the individual and unit level, were common in both the Republican Guard and the Popular Army, with little apparent enforcement of regulations. He carries a Romanian-made Type I AKM bayonet in a bayonet frog especially made by the Romanians for export to Iraq, even though his weapon is incapable of mounting it; as with most soldiers in most armies, bayonets were first and foremost a utility tool, only rarely seeing use as a fighting knife or fixed to a rifle's muzzle. His chest rig is a Chinese-made four-cell version supplied to Iraq, containing spare magazines for his 7.62×39mm Tabuk Short Assault Rifle, an Iraqi version of the AKS-74U carbine (*Ukorochenniy*; shortened) that was simply a truncated AKMS, achieving its reduction in size by combining the foresight and gas block (much as the Romanian PM md. 80 assault rifle had done). There was no fitting for a bayonet or cleaning rod, and it used the same 30-round AKM-style magazines as most other weapons in the Iraqi arsenal, though special 20-round magazines were also available. The Tabuk Short Assault Rifle was a desirable status symbol, and would likely most often be found in the hands of officers or SF units.

(2) Paratrooper, 68th Special Forces Brigade, Operation Karbala 5, January 1987

The paratrooper *'Arif* (sergeant) wears an imported French F1 jump helmet, one of a number of helmet designs used by Iraqi airborne troops that included the South Korean-manufactured M80-C helmet, an M80 variant specifically designed for paratroopers (the key difference being in the addition of 'A' yokes and a chin-cup to the helmet's strap). Other types of helmet worn by paratroopers included the standard M80, as well as the Polish Helm wz. 63. In common with many other airborne units, the Iraqis drew much of their inspiration from the British, adopting a near-identical maroon beret but adorned with a different style of jump wings in gold for the pin. The British influence extended to the uniform and equipment: his high-quality smock is inspired by the British Pattern 68 uniform in DPM, though this version was produced for Iraq under contract in Romania. His webbing is Pakistani-

manufactured Pattern 58, though, as with other branches of the Iraqi Army, great variation could be expected. He is armed with a Romanian 7.62×39mm PM md. 80 assault rifle, also known under its export designation as the AIMR. Like its inspiration, the AKS-74U, it was a very compact weapon with a side-folding stock; it normally used 20-round magazines but it could accept any AKM-style magazine, and like the other Romanian AKM variants (the fixed-stock PM md. 63 and folding-stock PM md. 65) it had a distinctive wooden pistol foregrip. Though paratroopers needed compact weapons its use here is as much about the status derived from carrying such a firearm as it is to do with its inherent capabilities, and there is little likelihood that the PM md. 80 saw widespread distribution even among elite units.

(3) LMG gunner, 2nd Commando Brigade, Operation Tawakkalna ala Allah, May 1988

This Iraqi Army commando wears a green beret, a legacy of the Army's commando units' connection with and training by British special forces including the Royal Marines; the rest of his uniform is modelled after the British tropical version, but in the official desert DPM pattern which the British had sold to Iraq in the latter part of the 1980s. Some of the original uniforms were of British manufacture, but later batches were either locally made or possibly outsourced to Romania (the Romanian company Pan East International made versions of British DPM-pattern smocks and trousers for export to the Iraqi regime throughout the 1980s). He wears a Chinese-made Pattern 58 belt, a Chinese-made Soviet-pattern ammunition pouch that could hold four 40-round magazines, and he carries a Yugoslavian-made M1 gas mask on his hip – a necessity amid an operation that freely deployed mustard gas and nerve agents to facilitate the advance of Iraqi forces. He is armed with a 7.62×39mm RPK (*Ruchnoy Pulemyot Kalashnikova*; Kalashnikov's hand-held machine gun), a variant of the AK-47/AKM assault rifle designed in the early 1960s that was intended to function as a squad light machine gun, replacing the RPD. Some modifications were made to the length of the receiver to decrease the rate of fire to something approaching 600rd/min; and a heavier, longer chromium-lined barrel improved accuracy and allowed greater periods of sustained fire before overheating. The barrel also came with a permanently affixed bipod that improved stability when prone, and the fact that it used the same-calibre ammunition and would take the same magazines as regular AKM-style assault rifles made for simpler logistics. Though it could be fitted with a 75-round drum, it was common to find the RPK using 40-round magazines.

Al-Faw Peninsula, 15 February 1986: a captured Iraqi soldier with a small photo of the Ayatollah Khomeini attached to his right breast pocket sits with other prisoner of war. The soldiers are mostly wearing the basic olive-green fatigues, but the man at the front also has a military-issue pullover, worn by both officers and men alike. (Kaveh Kazemi/Getty Images)

contribute little except mass to a modern war, so its personnel were largely used for secondary duties such as security around installations. Furthermore, the Popular Army was also a heavy drain on the civilian labour force, so its members tended to be deployed for just 2–3 months at a time, before returning to their civilian lives and employment. Thus parallels with the fanatical Iranian Pasdaran are actually somewhat limited.

National Defence Battalions

A distinctive element of Saddam's wider paramilitary forces were the National Defence Battalions (NDBs), which were distinctive in that they were formed from Iraq's Kurdish community, a people with a long-standing history of struggles against the Saddam regime. The NDBs, which came to number more than 250,000 personnel and 147 battalions by 1987, were manned by pro-regime Kurds and had been formed in the 1960s to support or engage in counter-insurgency operations against Kurdish rebel groups. A mixture of tribal warriors, police and light infantry, the NDBs during the Iran–Iraq War were commanded by the Directorate of Military Intelligence and the Army in the Northern Command, although the battalions themselves were headed by Kurdish tribal leaders, who also had a responsibility for recruitment.

As one might expect given the politically troubled nature of Kurdistan, the NDBs were a difficult force to manage. While they did engage in counter-insurgency operations, there was evidence of many fighters changing sides between the Kurds and the Iraqi forces. There was also very low morale and a high level of desertion, despite the fact that summary punishments for desertion could be brutal.

IRAQI WEAPONS AND EQUIPMENT

Iraq acquired its weapons, equipment and vehicles from a comprehensive list of international sources. The largest of these was the Soviet Union, with whom Iraq had struck a close supply relationship, but others included Czechoslovakia, France, China, Poland, Romania, Egypt, South Africa, Yugoslavia, Brazil and the United States. The diverse range of suppliers reflects the fact that Iraq managed to avoid Iran's fate of becoming a virtual pariah state on the international markets. Yet the way that the war brutally squeezed the Iraqi economy meant that Iraq couldn't always purchase top-end military items.

At the front-line infantry level, most soldiers were armed with directly purchased or (more commonly) budget copies of contemporary Soviet small arms – the AK-47/AKM assault rifle, SVD Dragunov sniper rifle, and the RPD, RPK, PK and DShK machine guns. A standard rifle was the Tabuk, a direct-licensed copy of the Yugoslavian Zastava second-pattern M70B1, produced in Iraq by the Al-Qadissiya Establishments factory east of Bir Musammad, Babil province, from 1980 onwards. Manufactured on machinery sourced from Yugoslavia, the Iraqi Tabuks lacked chromium lining in the bore like the early Zastava guns, while other aspects of quality control seem to have deteriorated over time, often resulting in shoddy and badly worn weapons. Iraq also had a total of 19 state ordnance factories manufacturing explosive items such as RPG-7 anti-tank rocket launchers, hand grenades and mines.

Iraqi armoured divisions and brigades (including the Republican Guard) together operated some 4,500 MBTs over the course of the war, mainly Soviet T-54, T-55, T-62 and T-72 types and Chinese Type 59,

29 February 1984: Iraqi soldiers armed with infantry squad support weapons strike an upbeat pose. Among the weapons on display here are an RPG and 7.62×39mm Al-Quds light machine guns, the latter being based upon the Yugoslavian Zastava M72, which was in turn a copy of the Soviet RPK. (Jacques Pavlovsky/ Sygma via Getty Images)

Iraqi troops guard a waterway, armed with a Soviet 23×152mm ZU-23-2 *Shilka* double-barrelled anti-aircraft autocannon. In combat, the ZU-23-2 was frequently used to engage infantry positions and light vehicles/armour as much as Iranian aircraft. It can fire high-explosive and armour-piercing ammunition types. These personnel wear khaki fatigues plus M80 helmets, the latter covered with leaf-like helmet netting. (Pierre PERRIN/Gamma-Rapho via Getty Images)

Type 69-I and Type 69-II types (all the Chinese vehicles were delivered between 1982 and 1987), but also small numbers (*c*.150) of British Chieftains. Lighter armour included about 100 Soviet PT-76 light tanks, but the main reconnaissance vehicles and infantry fighting vehicles (IFVs) were the BMP and BRDM-2 (Soviet Union), the FUG-70 (Hungary), the ERC-90 (France), the MOWAG Roland (Switzerland), and the EE-9 *Cascavel* and EE-3 *Jararaca* (Brazil). For APCs the Iraqi military relied upon the BTR-50/-60/-152 (Soviet Union), the OT-62 and OT-64 (Czechoslovakia), the M113A1 (United States), the Panhard M3 (France) and the EE-11 *Urutu* (Brazil).

For both towed and SP artillery, the Iraqis again used Soviet types, particularly the 122mm D-74, D-30 and M1938 (M30), 130mm M1954 (M46), 152mm M1937 (ML-20) towed howitzers and the 122mm 2S1 *Gvozdika* and 152mm 2S3 *Akatsiya* SP howitzers, although the SP types were available in relatively limited numbers. SP types from the United States (the 155mm M109 howitzer) and France (the 155mm AUF1 GCT gun) were also pressed into service, while other types and sources of towed artillery included the 105mm M56 Pack Howitzer (Italy), the 130mm Type 59-1 (a Chinese copy of the M46), the 155mm M114 (United States), the 155mm G5 (South Africa) and the 155mm GHN-45 (an Austrian-produced version of the Canadian GC-45).

The Iraqi forces used MLRS launchers to deliver area destruction, specifically the 122mm BM-21 *Grad* and 132mm BM-13/-16 *Katyusha* (Soviet Union), and the 127mm ASTROS II, 180mm ASTROS SS-40 and 300mm ASTROS SS-60 (Brazil). The most potent of its missile technologies, however, were the Soviet R-17E/SS-1b Scud-C (plus the local *al-Hussein* variant) and Luna-M/FROG-7, which together gave Iraqi ground forces a long-range strategic reach; they were operated by four surface-to-surface missile brigades. For anti-armour roles, the Iraqi forces used the Soviet AT-3 Sagger (both ground operated and vehicle mounted), the AT-4 Spigot and the French MILAN, plus a collection of recoilless rifles and 85mm, 100mm and 105mm anti-tank guns, while SAM systems included the Soviet S-75 *Dvina* (SA-2 Guideline), S-125 *Neva/Pechora* (SA-3 Goa), 9K31 *Strela-1* (SA-9 Gaskin), 9K32 *Strela-2* (SA-7 Grail) and 9K34 *Strela-3* (SA-14 Gremlin), and the Franco-German Roland. Air defence weaponry also includes a variety of autocannon types, such as the Soviet 23mm ZSU-23-4 *Shilka* and 57mm ZSU-57-2.

The *c*.280 helicopters used by Iraqi Army Aviation Corps were an eclectic bunch. Attack types included the Soviet Mi-24 Hind equipped with the AT-2 Swatter anti-armour missile; the French SA.342 Gazelle equipped with the Franco-German HOT missile (French: *Haut subsonique Optiquement Téléguidé Tiré d'un Tube*; High Subsonic, Optical, Remote-

Guided, Tube-Launched); the SA.321 Super Frelon, some of which were armed with Exocet missiles for anti-ship warfare; and the West German Bo 105 equipped with AS.11 ATGWs. For transportation and assault, the options were mainly the Soviet Mi-6 Hook, Mi-8 Hip and Mi-4 Hound, and the French SA.330 Puma.

The Republican Guard was known for receiving the best equipment available to Iraqi forces, at the expense of the regular Army. In the matter of tanks, for example, the Republican Guard armoured formations and units were given preferential access to imported T-72s, which were the most modern MBTs in the Iraqi arsenal. Some 1,200 T-72M/M-1s were imported from the Soviet Union, Czechoslovakia and Poland following the first years of the war, and many of these went to the Republican Guard. Yet while these were the best MBTs used by the Iraqis, they were not necessarily the most sophisticated pieces of armour on the international market, essentially being budget export models, with simplified armour and stripped of some of the more sophisticated fire-control systems of the most modern Soviet T-72s. Nevertheless, in the hands of well-trained crews the T-72M/M-1s were more than capable of taking on the best of the Iranian MBTs, the Chieftains, and gave a respectable 'punch' to Republican Guard offensive movements.

Another armoured vehicle used by the Republican Guard was the BMP-2 IFV, although in limited numbers – some 200 were ordered from the Soviet Union in 1986 and delivered over the final year of the war and into 1989. The Iraqi military in general had plentiful stocks of the BMP-1 IFV, which carried a three-man crew and eight passengers and was armed with a 73mm 2A28 *Grom* low-pressure smoothbore short-recoil semi-automatic gun plus a 9M14 *Malyutka* (AT-3 Sagger) ATGM launcher. The 1973 Yom Kippur War exposed the BMP-1's vulnerabilities in armour and deficiencies in firepower, and the BMP-2 consequently emerged as its improved successor, with slightly deeper armour and better armament in the form of a 30mm 2A42 autocannon and the 9P135M ATGM launcher, which could fire a broader range of missile types. On the artillery side of things, another key piece of Republican Guard equipment was the 2S1 *Gvozdika* SP gun, of which Iraq ordered 100 in 1986. Mounting a 122mm 2A18 howitzer (based on the D-30 towed howitzer), the 2S1 was fully amphibious (although such an asset had limited utility in the Middle East theatre) and had a gun range of 15.3km.

One particularly judicious vehicular investment made by the Iraqi armed forces was the purchase of some 1,500 tank transporters, plus large volumes of trucks. The upshot of these assets was improved front-line logistics and better cross-theatre mobility, particularly for the armoured divisions. The Iraqis also built major new road networks linking the fronts from north to south, meaning that the Iraqi armed forces could respond quickly to fresh Iranian offensives.

Saddam Hussein visits the front line during the Iran–Iraq War. This ZU-2 double-barrelled anti-aircraft gun fired 14.5×114mm ammunition, the round having been developed for the PTRS and PTRD anti-tank rifles fielded by the Soviet Union during World War II. (Scott Peterson/ Getty Images)

CONCLUSION

In 1991, the Iraqi Army – which by this time was one of the most combat-experienced military forces in the world – went to war against a massive and technologically advanced Coalition army, following Saddam Hussein's invasion and occupation of Kuwait the previous year. The outcome of this battle was almost bewilderingly one-sided. The liberation campaign lasted just four days, ending in an absolutely decisive Coalition victory with just over 1,100 Coalition casualties compared to more than 25,000 Iraqi casualties. Thousands of Iraqi armoured vehicles were destroyed and left to rust in the desert. Similarly, in 2003 the US-led invasion of Iraq crushed the conventional Iraqi military in less than six weeks (the subsequent insurgency was quite another matter).

The reasons why Iraq was able to sustain a war for eight long years with Iran, but could not prosecute a conflict against the United States, Britain and their allies for more than a few weeks are multi-layered and complex, as much to do with strategy and politics, the personality of Saddam Hussein, and post-1988 military changes, as they are about tactics and operations. One interesting perspective on Iraqi strengths and vulnerabilities comes from a US Strategic Studies Institute document, published just prior to the Coalition forces crossing the Iraqi and Kuwaiti borders, analysing the lessons to be learned from the Iran–Iraq War. Its summaries of Iraqi 'ground vulnerabilities' identified various shortcomings, including a lack of coordination across corps and other boundaries, the scarcity and vulnerability

Khorramshahr, 18 August 1988: a member of the IRGC is pictured at his post as the ceasefire ending the Iran–Iraq War begins. He wears a West German-style parka (a high-quality and sought-after item) and an M62 helmet. His firearm is an AKM-type assault rifle, either of Soviet, East German or Chinese origin. (Kaveh Kazemi/ Getty Images)

Baghdad, 20 August 1988: an elated Iraqi soldier celebrates after the arrival of United Nations peacekeeping forces, signalling the long-awaited ceasefire with Iran. The red lanyard and the triangular sleeve insignia indicate he is a member of the Republican Guard; red berets were worn by the Republican Guard (as were black berets), Military Police and airborne soldiers. (Bernard Bisson/Sygma via Getty Images)

of Iraqi lines of communication – albeit tempered by efficient engineering and logistical capabilities – and the poor quality of the Popular Army units that could be used to screen more seasoned Iraqi formations. The report also highlighted Iraqi tactical practices that could be identified and used to Coalition forces' advantage, such as the use of prepared killing zones and carefully prepared field defences, and emphasized that the Republican Guard units were likely to lead any counter-attacking effort (Pelletiere & Johnson 1991: 112–13). The Iraqi ground forces are characterized as powerful in the defence, with offensive and counter-attack capabilities concentrated in one particular formation (the Republican Guard), but with vulnerabilities in command and control, communications and leadership that left them open to fast-manoeuvre exploitations.

Had the report been extended to include the Iranian armed forces, the analysis would have had a different set of parameters, but the ultimate conclusions might have gravitated towards similar principles. The Iranian military during the Iran–Iraq War was offensively minded, often to the complete disregard of the human cost, but with a talent in infantry infiltration and assault tactics in the face of a defensively capable opponent. Iranian troops fought well at night and over rough terrain, and their levels of offensive motivation were generally higher than those of the Iraqis. Like the Iraqi forces, however, the Iranians had vulnerabilities in command and control (especially in combined-arms synchronization and devolved decision-making), and they often struggled with poor logistical flow and inadequate coordination of armour and artillery support. Ultimately, neither side really seemed to have a clear sense of how to fight a modern war, based on sound doctrines and integrated technology, delivered through well-trained soldiers across the board. The prioritization of ideological bodies such as the Pasdaran, Basij and Republican Guard was also arguably to the detriment of the wider armies. Finally, both Iran and Iraq had leaders who were profoundly unmoved by mass casualties, and who placed attrition at the heart of their warfighting. As history largely tells us, attrition alone ultimately accomplishes little except spilling oceans of blood.

FURTHER READING

Al-Lihaibi, Macdh Ayed (1989). *An Analysis of the Iran-Iraq War: Military Strategy and Political Objectives*. Montgomery, AL: Air War College, US Air Force.

Al-Maharashi, Ibrahim & Salama, Sammy (2008). *Iraq's Armed Forces: An analytical history*. London: Routledge.

Center for Strategic and International Studies (n.d.). 'III. The strengths and weaknesses, economic factors, force strengths, and other military factors that shaped the course of the war'. 9005lessonsiraniraqii-chap03.pdf

Connell, Michael (2013). *Iranian Operational Decision Making: Case Studies from the Iran–Iraq War*. Washington, DC: CNA Strategic Studies.

Global Security (2011). 'People's Army/Popular Army/People's Militia (Al Jaysh ash Shaabi)'. https://www.globalsecurity.org/military/world/iraq/militia.htm

Global Security (2021). 'Army/Islamic Iranian Ground Forces (IIGF)'. https://www.globalsecurity.org/military/world/iran/army.htm

Hooten, E.R., Cooper, Tom & Nadimi, Farzin (2016). *The Iran–Iraq War – Volume 1: The Battle for Khuzestan, September 1980–May 1982*. Solihull: Helion.

It was only in the latter stages of the Iran–Iraq War that Saddam Hussein finally realized he had to give his senior officers some more leeway in command if they were to gain the advantage over the Iranians. Here, Colonel-General Adnan Khairallah, Iraq's Minister of Defence and Saddam Hussein's brother-in-law, confers with senior officers during the conflict. (PD/Creative Commons)

Hooten, E.R., Cooper, Tom & Nadimi, Farzin (2017). *The Iran–Iraq War – Volume 3: Iraq's Triumph*. Solihull: Helion & Company Ltd.

Hooten, E.R., Cooper, Tom & Nadimi, Farzin (2018). *The Iran–Iraq War – Volume 4: The Forgotten Fronts*. Solihull: Helion & Company Ltd.

Hooten, E.R., Cooper, Tom & Nadimi, Farzin (2019). *The Iran–Iraq War – Volume 2: Iran Strikes back, June 1982–December 1986*. Solihull: Helion.

Huggins, William D. (1994). 'The Republican Guards and Saddam Hussein's Transformation of the Iraqi Army'. *Arab Studies Journal*, vol. 2, no. 1, Spring 1994.

Karsh, Efraim (2002). *The Iran–Iraq War, 1980–88*. Essential Histories 20. Oxford: Osprey Publishing.

Pelletiere, Stephen C. & Johnson III, Douglas V. (1991). *Lessons Learned: The Iran–Iraq War*. Carlisle Barracks, PA: Strategic Studies Institute, US Army War College.

Pinkley, Brandon A. (2018). *Guarding History: The Islamic Revolutionary Guard Corps and the Memory of the Iran–Iraq War*. Washington, DC: Joint History Office of the Chairman of the Joint Chiefs of Staff.

Pivka, Otto von (1979). *Armies of the Middle East*. London: Book Club Associates.

Roberts, Mark (1996). *Khomeini's Incorporation of the Iranian Military*, McNair Paper 48. Washington, DC: National Defense University.

Schahgaldian, Nikola B. (1987). *The Iranian Military Under the Islamic Republic*. Santa Monica, CA: The RAND Corporation.

Wehrey, Frederic et al. (2009). *The Rise of the Pasdaran: Assessing the Domestic Roles of Iran's Islamic Revolutionary Guards Corps*. Santa Monica, CA: The RAND Corporation.

Wilson, Ben (2007). 'The Evolution of Iranian Warfighting During the Iran–Iraq War: When Dismounted Light Infantry Made the Difference'. *Infantry*, July–August 2007.

Woods, Kevin M., Murray, Williamson & Holiday, Thomas (2009). *Saddam's War: An Iraqi Military Perspective of the Iran–Iraq War*, McNair Paper 70. Washington, DC: Institute for National Strategic Studies, National Defense University.

This preserved section of battlefield at Fath-Olmobin, Shush, Iran – the scene of major combat in 1982 – gives a good impression of the static lines over which the Iran–Iraq War was frequently fought. High earthen banks and berms gave good protection against artillery fire. (Ninara/CC BY 2.0/ Creative Commons)

INDEX

References to illustrations are shown in **bold**. Plates are shown with page locators in brackets.

Abadan/Ahvaz, fighting for 6, **26**, **33**, 36, **37**
air-defence forces: (Iran) 17, 32; (Iraq) 37, 58
air-to-surface missiles: (Iran) 24; (Iraq) 59
airborne forces: (Iran) 8, 30, **D1(31)**; (Iraq) 37, 44, 54, **H2(55)**
al-Faw Peninsula, fighting for 5, 6, 19, 38, **E3(39)**, 43, 52, 56
al-Howeizah/Amara, fighting for 6, 41, 53
anti-aircraft guns: (Iran) 29, 32; (Iraq) 59
anti-armour bdes/cos: (Iran) 17; (Iraq) 47
anti-armour missiles (Iraq) 58–59
anti-tank bns (Iraq) 47
anti-tank guided missiles: (Iran) 20, **B1(21)**, 24, **C2(25)**, 29, 29, 30, 32; (Iraq) 50, 58, 59
anti-tank guns/rifles (Iraq) 58, 59
anti-tank rocket launchers: (Iran) 24, 32; (Iraq) **40**, 57, **57**
armoured fighting vehicles (Iran) 12
armoured forces: (Iran) 12, 20, 24, 61; (Iraq) 35, 43, 52, 59
  bns/cos: (Iran) 8; (Iraq) 37, 47
  bdes/dvns: (Iran) 8, 10, 17, 24, **C1(25)**; (Iraq) 35, 36–37, 47, 50, **G1(51)**, 52, 57, 59
    tank crews: (Iran) 24, **C1(25)**; (Iraq) 50, **G1(51)**
    tanks: (Iran) 12, 24, 29, 30, 32, 58, 59; (Iraq) 20, 24, 37, 43, 50, 57, 58, 59
armoured personnel carriers: (Iran) 29; (Iraq) 37, 58
artillery forces: (Iran) 8, 12, 20, 36, 42, 61; (Iraq) 35, 36, 52
  bns/bdes: (Iran) 8, 10, 17; (Iraq) 37, 47
  groups (Iran) 8, 10
artillery pieces: (Iran) 8, 10, 14, 17, 29, 30, 32; (Iraq) 47, 58, 59

Basij (the) 5, 6, 18, 20, **B2–3(21)**, 22–24, **22**, **23**, 24, **24**, 26, 27, 28, 32, 61
Basra/Bostan/Bubiyan Is., fighting for 6, 13

chemical decontamination bdes (Iran) 17
  jackets/suits 19, **23**, 24, 32
chemical-defence bns (Iraq) 37
chemical-warfare teams (Iraq) 32
chemical weapons, use of (Iraq) 5, 6, 14, 19, 24, 32, 43, 44, 50, 54
commando forces (Iraq) 37, 44
corps (Iraq) 36–37, 43, 46

engineer forces: (Iran) 8, 17; (Iraq) 37, 47
equipment/kit (Iran) **10**, 14, **A1**, 3(15), **16**, **18**, **19**, 20, **B2–3(21)**, 22, 23, 24, **C1–2(25)**, 30, **D1–3(31)**, 32
equipment/kit (Iraq) 22, **36**, **37**, 38, **E1**, 3(39), 41, 42, 43, 44, **F1–2(45)**, 47, 48, 49, 50, **G2(51)**, 54, **H1, 3(55)**, 57

female fighters (Iran) 24, 26, 27, 28, **28**: Sisters of Zenyab 28

Gendarmerie (Iran) 28
Ghalollah paramilitary group 28
grenadiers (Iraq) 38, **E1(39)**

Halabja, fighting for 6
hand grenades (Iraq) 50, **G2(51)**, 57
headwear (Iran): bandannas 5, 6, 17, 20, **22**, **23**, 24, **C2(25)**, 26, 27, 28; berets

30, **D1(31)**; caps **19**, 20, **B3(21)**, 24, 30, **D3(31)**; helmets 9, **10**, **11**, 14, **A1** 3(15), 16, 18, 19, 20, **B1–2(21)**, 24, **C1**, 3(25), 30, **D2(31)**, 33, 33
headwear (Iraq): berets 35, 36, 37, 40, 44, **F3(45)**, 52, 54, **H1(55)**, 59, 61, 62; caps 36, 43, 59; helmets 34, 35, 36, 38, **E1–3(39)**, 40, 41, 42, 43, 44, **F1–2(45)**, 46, 47, 48, 49, 50, **G1–3(51)**, 53, 53, 54, **H2(55)**, 57, 58, 60, 61
Hussein, Saddam 4, 5, 34, 35, 37, 40–41, 44, 46, 48–49, **52**, 53, 56, 59, 60, **62**

Imperial Iranian Army 8, **8**, 11, 14, 30
infantry bdes/dvns: (Iran) 8, 10, 14, **A3(15)**, 17; (Iraq) 36, 37, 38, **E1–3(39)**, 46, 52
infantry bns/cos: (Iran) 17; (Iraq) 37
infantry fighting vehicles (Iraq) 37, 58, 59
Iraqi Army
  casualties/losses 13, 29, 41
  composition/strength 35, 36–37, 38, 40, 43, 46, 52
  conscription 38, 40
  morale/desertion 41
  operational shortcomings 35, 40
  recruitment/recruits/training 34, 35, 38, 40, 41, **42**, 47, 48
  and Republican Guard 44, 46, 47, 48, 49, 50, 59
  and Saddam Hussein 34, 35, 40–41
Iraqi Army Aviation Corps 37, 58:
  helicopters/crews 50, **G3(51)**, 52, 58–59
Iraqi Border Guard 53
Iraqi Republican Guard 35, **35**, 36, 43, 44, **F1–3(45)**, 46–50, **46**, **49**, **G1(51)**, 52, 54, **H1(55)**, 57, 59, 60, 61, **61**
Islamic Republic of Iran Air Force 19
Islamic Republic of Iran Army
  casualties/losses 13, 14
  command and control 10–11, 12–13, 61
  composition/strength 8, 10, 11
  conscription 12
  doctrine/tactics 12–13, 14, 43, 61
  effects of Islamic Revolution 11, 12
  operational shortcomings 11–14, 61
  recruitment/recruits/training 11–12, 14
  and Revolutionary Guard Corps 14, 19, 20
Islamic Republic of Iran Army Aviation 8, 10, 29: helicopters/crews 10, 24, **C3(25)**
Islamic Republic of Iran Navy 19, **29**, 30, 43
Islamic Revolutionary Guard Corps 8, 10, 14, 16, **16**, 17, **17**, 18–19, **19**, 20, 22, 23, 26, 28, 30, **D3(31)**, 32

Jondollah paramilitary organization (Iran) 28

Khomeini, Ayatollah (the) 4, 5, 8, 10, **11**, 12, 16, 17, 22, 23, 56
Khorramshahr, fighting for 4, 6, 14, **A1(15)**, 28, 30, **D2(31)**, 34, 36, 38, **E2(39)**
Khuzestan province, fighting for 4, 6
Kurdish forces/rebels 4, 35, 56
Kurdistan, fighting for 6, 28, 38, 56

machine-gunners/guns: (Iran) 12, 14, **A2(15)**, 25, **26**, 29, 32; (Iraq) 38, **E2(39)**, 44, **F2(45)**, 54, **H3(55)**, 57, **57**
machine pistols (Iraq) 50, **G1(51)**
Majnoon Is./Mehran/Musian, fighting for 6
mechanized bdes/dvns: (Iran) 10, 17; (Iraq) 36, 37, 44, **F1–2(45)**, 50, **G2(51)**
mechanized infantry bns/bdes: (Iran) 8, 17, 24, **C2(25)**; (Iraq) 37, 47, 52

mechanized infantry dvns: (Iran) 10; (Iraq) 50, **G2(51)**
missile operators (Iran) 20, **B1(21)**
MLRS forces/launchers: (Iran) 10, 32; (Iraq) 58
mortar cos/teams: (Iran) **33**; (Iraq) 37
mortars: (Iran) 12, 32, **33**; (Iraq) 37, 54

National Defence Battalions (Iraq) 56
naval commandos/infantry (Iran) 17, **29**, 30, **D2–3(31)**

Pahlavi, Mohammad Reza (Shah) 8, 14, 30
Pasdaran (Iran) 11, 12, 14, 16–20, **17**, 18, **B1(21)**, 22, 23, 24, 30, 32, 35, 53, 56, 61
pistols: (Iran) 20, **B3(21)**, 24, **C1**, 3(25); (Iraq) 44, **F3(45)**, 50, **G3(51)**
Popular Army (Iraq) 35, 44, 53–54, 56, 61

Qasr-e Shirin, fighting for 6

radiomen/radios: (Iran) 12, 19, 30, **D3(31)**; (Iraq) 44, **F1(45)**
ranks/rank insignia: (Iran) 11, **11**, 12, **A1(15)**, 20, **B1(21)**, 24, **C1(25)**, 30; (Iraq) **40**, 44, 50, **G1(51)**, 52, 54, 62
recoilless rifles: (Iran) 32; (Iraq) 58
reconnaissance forces/vehicles: (Iran) 17, 29; (Iraq) 37, 47, 58
rifle cos/pltns/squads (Iraq) 37
rifle grenades (Iraq) 38, **E1(39)**, 50
rifles: (Iran) 8, 24; (Iraq) 35, 37, **40**
  assault rifles: (Iran) 8, 20, **B1–2(21)**, 22, 23, 24, **C2(25)**, 28, **28**, 30, **D3(31)**; (Iraq) 34, **34**, 36, 38, **E1(39)**, 41, 42, 43, 44, **F3(45)**, 46, 48, 49, 50, **G2(51)**, 54, **H1–2(55)**, 57, 60
  battle rifles: (Iran) 9, **10**, 14, **A1**, 3(15), 16, 25, 27, 29, 30, **D1(31)**, 32, **32**
  sniper rifles: (Iraq) 38, **E3(39)**, 57
rocket-launcher batteries (Iraq) 47

SAM systems (Iran) 29, 30, 32, (Iraq) 58
Sarollah paramilitary group (Iran) 28
Shalamcheh, fighting for 6
Shatt al-Arab (the), fighting for 4, 13, **29**, 30, **D3(31)**, 37
signals units: (Iran) 8; (Iraq) 37
Special Forces units: (Iran) 8, 10, **29**, 30, **D1–3(31)**; (Iraq) 37, 43, 44, 46, 47, 54, **H1–3(55)**
submachine guns (Iran) 30, **D2(31)**
Supreme Defence Council (Iran) 10, 11
surface-to-surface missile bdes (Iraq) 58
surface-to-surface missiles (Iraq) 58
Susangerd, fighting for 6

transportation units: (Iran) 8; (Iraq) 37
  transporters/trucks (Iraq) 37, 50, 59

Umm Qasr, fighting for 32
uniforms/clothing camouflage patterns 41, 46, 47, 48, 49, 61: 'brushstroke' 14, 20, **B2(21)**, 30, **D2(31)**, 42, 44, **F1(45)**, 54, **H1(55)**; DPM 14, 30, **D1(31)**, 38, **E3(39)**, 54, **H2–3(55)**; 'island' 18; leaf 44; 'lizard' 14, **A2(15)**, 44; 'Panther'/'spot' 14, **A3(15)**, 20, **B1(21)**; 'puzzle spot' 20, **B3(21)**; 'ragged leaf' 37; 'vertical stripe' 44, **F3(45)**, 'waves' 44, **F1(45)**